Learning to Learn

Learning to Learn

How to help children get the best start on their lifelong learning journey

Sally Featherstone

BLOOMSBURY
LONDON • NEW DELHI • NEW YORK • SYDNEY

Bloomsbury Education

An imprint of Bloomsbury Publishing Plc

50 Bedford Square	1385 Broadway
London	New York
WC1B 3DP	NY 10018
UK	USA

www.bloomsbury.com

Bloomsbury is a registered trademark of Bloomsbury Publishing Plc

First published 2014

British Library Cataloguing-in-Publication Data
A catalogue record for this book is available from the British Library.

ISBN: PB: 978-1-4729-0608-3
       ePub: 978-1-4729-0734-9
       ePDF: 978-1-4729-0735-6

Library of Congress Cataloging-in-Publication Data
A catalog record for this book is available from the Library of Congress.

10 9 8 7 6 5 4 3 2 1

Acknowledgements
We would like to thank the staff and children at Little Angel School House and LEYF for their time and patience in helping with the photographs in this book.

Other photographs reproduced with the kind permission of Sally Featherstone, Phill Featherstone and Sam Goodman.

Typeset by Newgen Knowledge Works (P) Ltd., Chennai, India
Printed and bound by CPI Group (UK) Ltd, Croydon CR0 4YY

Some thanks

In this book, which has explored the things I consider most important in the early years of education, I wish to add some words of thanks.

Firstly, I want to thank my husband and partner, Phill, who has been by my side for more years that either of us can count, and has recognised and supported my unique writing style, which starts with hours of apparently doing absolutely nothing except staring at the view from the top of our hill while he wonders if I'm ever going to put a single word into print. He then tries valiantly to find space for coffee cups and wine glasses among toppling piles of reference books on every flat surface of the house, while I engage in a flurry of Internet use, with frequent incidents where I say 'Did you know…?', and 'That's really interesting.' Then he endures with patience my two fingered typing skills and occasional inappropriate language as I pour out several months of preparation in frantic weeks of writing, finally reading my drafts for me, and making just the right number of helpful comments to preserve my sense of achievement, while ensuring I don't make too many errors and hopefully meet my deadlines. I could not manage any of my work without him.

And of course, without the thousands of children I have been privileged to meet in my long career; along with their wonderfully inspiring teachers and practitioners, and their loving if sometimes less than perfect parents, I would have nothing to inspire my writing. Children hold a fascination, which will never fail to captivate me – from Alan in West Ham, trying and failing time and time again to tackle *Janet and John* with the aid of his pebble thick glasses; to Nicky, from a housing estate in Leicester, crouched under a table in my office, shouting abuse as he recovered from his latest tantrum; Charlotte, proudly bringing me a cake she had baked on her own at home; Damian who would only speak when I had my back to him; Mark, in care and trying valiantly to manage his own disappointment with what life has given him; Patrick, standing in the holly bush to take his mind off the desire to hit his best friend; or Nicola, suddenly discovering that she could read, when yesterday she couldn't. My contacts with these children, and all the others I have met, inspired me to read, research and talk about what is really important in the lives of young children as they struggle to make sense of the world. I thank each one of them.

Sally Featherstone 2014

Contents

Introduction

"'Live as if you were to die tomorrow. Learn as if you were to live forever.'"

Mahatma Gandhi

This book is about learning to learn, getting the learning bug, and keeping it for life. I believe this is one of the greatest gifts adults can give to children. There is no quick fix or easy way to help children to learn: deep, permanent learning follows immersion in exploring and thinking about the world and everything in it, ideally accompanied by adults who can support without taking over, inspire without overwhelming, and enlighten without overburdening.

For just over 100 years scientists have been investigating our genetic make-up to find out what makes us uniquely human, how our genes differ from those of animals, and which bits of the genome trigger brain cells to make links when we think. The Human Genome Project (HGP), in unpacking the genetic make-up of humans, has provided us with a vast amount of information about what makes each one of us different from every other human being on the Earth – even identical twins have significant numbers of differences in their individual genomes. As well as controlling visible features, our genetic make-up may include indicators of significant illnesses, weaknesses or talents.

Now we have all this knowledge, the frightening thing is how much of what we will be is determined at the moment of our conception, when a set of genes from each of our parents meet, and the battle for dominance between chromosomes ends in a unique embryo, different even from other children from the same parents. In this fraction of a second, many of the important things that will happen to us during our lives are decided – not just the colour of our eyes and hair or whether we will be a boy or a girl. More important than that, many illnesses and medical problems, including Autism, Attention Deficit Hyperactivity Disorder and, in some people, even cancer have a genetic trigger. We now know that many of the conditions that affect children are also proven to be genetic, although, when everyone has the potential trigger for Autism for example, we still don't know why it is only switched for some children.

The work on the genome has increased our knowledge of ourselves and how the human body works, but does this affect the traditional see-saw of thinking about nature and nurture? And what does it mean to those of us involved in education? Should we now accept that there is little we can do to affect children's futures, that nature will take its course, and that whether a child succeeds or fails has already been decided – can we just sit back and let their lives unfold?

How our genes affect our learning

Groups such as the Environmental Genome Project are looking at how genes are affected by substances and other factors in the environment – why it is that some people who smoke get cancer and some don't, whether it's a gene that protects one man from the harmful chemicals he works with, but makes his brother susceptible. These genes – susceptibility genes – respond differently to external factors. We may soon be able to identify which genes influence our ability to engage with learning, and retain what we learn.

What makes one child interested in words and reading, another in science? What is it that helps one child to concentrate while another is so easily distracted? Is it nature (our genes), or nurture (the environment) that makes us able to learn? And can we do anything to make sure that children get the best start in learning for life? Or have we really lost the race before they are born?

Well, if the race is already lost, parents and teachers all over the world can give up. If there was nothing we could do, there would be no point in trying to help any children but the brightest, most able learners, and we would focus our finest teachers and our financial investment on just those children, leaving the less genetically well-endowed to survive as they can. We do have some politicians who see this future as the right way to go. They ask, why invest in the children with doubtful heritage and less promising genomes, when you can nurture a 'master class' of adults educated according to their genome. Are we that far away from the brave new world of genetic engineering, not this time of sweetcorn or tomatoes, but of babies?

Nurture and culture

This book is for readers who want to make a difference, not by ignoring what the HGP is telling us, but by enhancing children's futures through other influences, those of nurture and culture.

Nurture

Nurture isn't just the loving care of a family, or the early support in nursery and the early years of school, it means looking at all the support mechanisms, from diet to the culture in a classroom, engaging with individuals, finding their strengths and interests and giving them the best possible start in life. Making sure they are ready and able to learn can make a huge difference to their futures. Parents and other family members, early years practitioners and teachers all have a part to play in the long path of learning to learn. Diet, exercise, stimuli for the brain, managing stress, company, friends, talk, singing and rhythm, can all contribute to improving young children's health and readiness for early learning. Of course, as they get older, they can play a part themselves by understanding how to learn, and exploring thinking skills.

Culture

Culture is not just what children see and hear in the media, or the influence of the community where they live. It's how the culture of learning sits within the school and home community. Is learning something that parents see as a welcome thing, or something they remember as unhelpful or unsuccessful? Do parents feel empowered to help their children? Do they feel welcome and confident when they meet their child's teacher or key person? The value that families and the local community place on education has as much effect on school success as the child's individual genetic profile. Investigating learning styles in isolation will not be as successful as embedding learning within the family and the community. Using cultural influences to spark interest and ensure relevance to children's lives outside the setting or school is an essential part of the role of any educator.

Using this book

In this book, I take a journey from conception to the eighth year of childhood, pausing sometimes to look at an aspect of learning which needs a bit more detail. I start with the unborn child – not because I think my readers are all intending to become parents, but unless we start from the beginning, we'll never get it right. In Scotland, the guidance for early years practitioners is called 'Pre-birth to Three', and emphasises that the nine months before birth are vital months, not simply for the growing body, but the developing brain. Early intervention studies are clear in their conclusions that how a mother eats, sleeps, works, plays and behaves in the months before her baby is born will have a significant influence on the future chances for her child.

I will explore the impact of the outside world on unborn babies, and what parents can do to affect how their baby behaves and responds, making connections in their brains even before birth, connections that will affect their early learning while they are in the womb, and after they are born. I will use simple explanations to show what is happening inside children's brains in the early months and years, as they try to understand the world about them, wrestle with language, become an explorer in their homes and gardens, and in local parks and playgrounds, and begin to make sense of their emotions.

In further chapters I will consider how the growing child begins to interact with the outside world, learning at home, in the community and later, in nursery and primary school. Learning to talk, learning to move with confidence, making friends, pretending and playing are all learning challenges for young children, who need supportive and knowledgeable

adults to help them. I will also consider the problems associated with a poor start in life, where learning is overtaken by just surviving.

Case studies

We know a lot about how children learn. How can we use this knowledge to make sure that every child can be the best learner possible? I am relying for illustration of the stages in learning on some case studies – stories of children who are helping me (and I hope you) to unpick the differences between children who have a 'fertile seed bed' to grow in and those who do not. These stories are not about individual, real children, they are illustrations, just as the illustrations in a storybook are not reality, but a prop for both reader and writer in understanding the story better. The children exemplify stages in the development of thinking and of learning, and in each chapter you will hear a little about one of these children's lives. This is followed by an unpicking of the key features of learning at this stage, to show what is happening in their brains and bodies, and how adults can make a difference to their futures.

Interludes on child development

Between the children's stories I have written some 'interludes', short pieces on specific aspects of child development; how exercise, nutrition and chemicals can affect learning and the growth of bodies and brains. I also offer some thoughts on thinking skills, learning styles, and the importance of helping children to concentrate and pay attention as they learn. The influence of our genetic make-up is a subject of great interest at the moment, and I have looked at the latest discussions on the balance between nature and nurture. I hope that reading the interludes will deepen your understanding of the learning process, and help you to enhance the lives of the children you work or live with.

The book has been written in the chronological order of a child's growth, but you may choose to dip into those parts which interest you most, and I hope you will be able to follow the narrative of *Learning to Learn* from whichever starting point you choose.

Stage 1 Before the beginning – Max is minus one month

'A grand adventure is about to begin.'

Winnie the Pooh (A.A. Milne)

Max is still in Angie's womb. He won't be born for a few weeks, but his brain is already growing and developing. He has a 100 billion brain cells safely protected in his skull. Each of these cells looks like a cross between a sea urchin and a Koosh ball – squidgy, and ready for action. Some of Max's brain cells have already reached out to link with other cells, beginning a process that will continue for years, only slowing down in late adulthood, but never stopping entirely. These cells, stimulated by signals from within his body or from outside, are linking and sending messages – there goes one that reaches far into his body to ensure that he is warm; and there goes another, responding to the theme music of his mother's favourite TV programme. She's sitting down now, resting with a cup of coffee, and unconsciously making calming endorphins, chemicals that flood Max in the womb, making him calm and content as well. As she sits, dozing and watching, she gently strokes the bump that is her child, and talks softly to him. He can recognise her voice already, as he can the voices of his dad Dale and his sister Carly, a three year old whirlwind, who races in at the end of her day at nursery to put her face next to her mum's bump, telling her new brother what she has been doing.

Mum's healthy diet

Max has also developed some preferences for foods and drinks, based on the diluted essences of these that flavour the amniotic fluid surrounding him – establishing likes and dislikes that will last for the whole of his life. Max gulps several mouthfuls of this fluid every day, establishing those preferences based on what Angie eats. This influence will be intensified by the flavours in the milk he drinks during breastfeeding. A wide and varied diet in pregnancy is likely to result in a baby who is prepared to try new foods and develop a broad nutritional palette.

Babies are hard wired to like salt and sugar, but more complex flavours such as vegetables may not be as easy to introduce, so it's worth getting them used to these flavours as young as possible, and the womb is a good place to start. Even if Angie didn't like vegetables, she would be well advised to eat them during pregnancy, not just for her own health, but for her baby's future fitness.

This is important because vegetables are building blocks for brain development. Children who eat those magical five fruits and vegetables every day really do get on better at school, and the building blocks for potential are laid down in the womb. Although she doesn't have much money, Angie buys and eats as much fresh fruit and vegetables as she can afford, shopping around now she is on maternity leave from her job.

A healthy lifestyle

Max is lucky. His mum doesn't smoke, and has kept her drinking levels low during her pregnancy, but many of her friends are different. They say that their enjoyment of alcohol, tobacco and even soft drugs are so central to their lives that they can't give them up. They may know that they are risking permanent damage to their babies, but their attitudes are self-centred, and many of them think that babies don't really have any needs before they are born. Angie heard on the TV recently that pregnant mums who take moderate exercise for 20 minutes, three times a week during their pregnancy can boost their baby's brain development, so she has decided to take this research seriously, and although she can't afford to go to the gym, she goes for a brisk walk three mornings a week, whatever the weather. This takes determination, as it's sometimes easier to stay under the duvet.

Angie is interested in Max's growth, even now, before he is born, and she keeps up with recent ideas on parenting by visiting parenting websites. She knows that if she talks to him and sings him nursery rhymes and her favourite pop songs, this will help his development. She moves gently as she sings along to the radio, keeping the rhythm of the music

Angie, Dale and Carly spend lots of time together in the early evenings and at weekends, but they can't afford to go to expensive restaurants, children's entertainments, films or theme parks. Instead, they go for walks in the local parks and woods, visit Dale's parents who live nearby, or occasionally splash out on fish and chips or a take-away curry.

Although they haven't done much reading about babies before birth, Angie and Dale have heard that high levels of stress, neglect or poor nourishment of the mother can all affect the development of their baby, producing stress chemicals that damage the brain. They know that they aren't perfect and there are disagreements in every family, but they try to keep their home stress free – almost impossible with a three year old among them – because they do know that if Max has a stress free time before he is born he will be a calmer, less anxious baby, sleeping better and with less likelihood of having baby problems such as colic.

Max's amazing brain

Max's parents have done all they can to make sure that his brain is protected from harm, and can develop in the best way possible.

The brain is an enormously complex network of billions of neurons, which by the time we are adults are connected by more than 90,000 miles of nerve fibres. This intricate structure allows us to absorb information quickly and efficiently.

A good way to think about the structure of the brain is to hold up your left arm vertically, resting on your elbow, with your fingers in a fist. Your arm and wrist represent the brain stem and the top of the spinal column. This is the oldest part of the brain, the remnant of our link with other animals. It is often referred to as our 'old reptilian brain', a useful description, as this is exactly what it does in humans. It controls the sort of things reptiles do – for instance breathing, blinking, swallowing, biting, which are often referred to as reflexes. It also controls our response to stress and danger in a reflex way – defending, attacking or running away.

Autonomic functions

The first parts of Max's baby brain to develop were the controls for his basic functions, called autonomic functions – heartbeat, breathing (underwater at first), responding to chemical signals, things Max will be able to do without thinking. These will continue to develop, so that as soon as he is born (and for some months before) he will be able to use his senses. He will be able to breathe, eat, sleep, cry, and use his sense of sight, smell, hearing and touch to recognise the people close to him, all without consciously thinking about it. Although at first his senses may be a bit confused and loud noises are 'seen', or bright lights 'felt'. The autonomic functions will be fully developed by the time Max is born, and under extreme pressure, Max, like all other humans may shut down his rational, thinking brain and revert to the 'fright or flight' response triggered in this part of his brain.

The limbic system

The next layer of Max's brain to develop was the limbic system. To see where this is, hold your arm up again and look at your fist. This part of the brain is the mid-brain, sometimes called the 'old mammalian brain', and it is wrapped round the top of Max's old reptilian brain. It's mainly involved with his feelings and emotions, such as joy, fear, anger and surprise. The reptilian and mammalian brains are common to all mammals.

Located within this part of the brain is the amygdala, which will eventually enable Max to control his 'flight/fight/freeze' response by preventing threat messages from passing down into his old reptilian brain. Of course, babies and young children need to practise controlling their emotions, and their old mammalian instincts are much closer to the surface than in adults. As Max grows and matures, with the help of his family and friends, he will learn to manage his feelings, and keep his thinking in the rational part of his brain, the cerebrum, which covers his mid-brain.

The mid-brain also contains the sites where Max will store his long-term memories. One of these specialised places is the cerebellum, which controls some aspects of learning, as it responds to and to some extent controls movement throughout the body. The cerebellum also has a key role in managing memory across the brain. The site in Max's brain which manages movement is very near the part of his brain that engages with learning and remembering.

The magical cerebrum

However, it is the third and final part of the brain that makes Max and the rest of us uniquely human

At this point you need to cup your right hand over your left fist. This final layer of the brain is the cerebrum, covered by the cerebral cortex. The cerebrum is the largest and most complex part of Max's brain, wrapping round the older parts of his brain, and covered by the cerebral cortex. As it grows, the surface of Max's cerebral cortex will expand and crinkle into furrows, but at the moment, it is as smooth as the back of your hand. Max's cerebrum and cerebral cortex are starting to work together as his human computer, enabling him eventually to think, imagine, debate, construct, empathise and all the other things that make us human, and most importantly, our unique ability to use language and symbols.

Cortex is the Greek word for the bark of a tree, and describes the surface of the adult brain very well. In the womb, and for the first months of his life, Max's cerebral cortex is smooth, because the brain cells it contains have made very few links with each other. It's the linking fibres between the cells that take up space. As Max learns things, his brain will get filled up with these new links that need more space, so the cerebrum has to expand to make room for all the new links. Our heads would be huge if the cerebral cortex didn't also crinkle to allow more links to fit into the skull. If you spread out an adult cerebral cortex, it would cover an average office desk, but usually, the cortex is crinkled up into the shape of a walnut half.

Even before he is born, Max has about 100 billion brain cells (neurons), almost all he will ever need. Scientists now think that humans continue to produce small numbers of new brain cells throughout their lives, particularly in the part of the brain that deals with memory, but the cells Max has now are really all he needs. Most of the rapid physical growth of Max's brain during early childhood will consist of making links between his neurons. His brain will double in size in his first year, and by the time he is three his brain will be 90% of its adult volume, with the physical growth being entirely in the wiring between cells. This growth is particularly rapid in the early months and years, and soon Max's brain will take on that double-sided walnut-half shape we all recognise.

A brain of two halves

Like every other human brain, Max's brain is formed in two similar shaped halves, joined from front to back by a thick connecting strip of fibres called the corpus callosum. The corpus callosum is a bridge of nervous tissue that connects the two hemispheres of the brain, allowing communication between the brain cells in the right brain and those in the left. It looks like a centipede with thousands of legs! See www.humanconnectomeproject. org for some amazing pictures.

This superhighway linking the right and left brains enables us to coordinate both thinking and movement, interpreting and passing on messages throughout the body. The number of links in the brains of newborn boys and girls is about the same, but, being a male, the links already formed in Max's brain will tend to be between neurons in one half or the other, seldom crossing the corpus callosum. On the other hand, many girls start to explore the bridge through the corpus callosum before birth, making links in both sides, even before they are born, so at birth their corpus callosum is often physically bigger than it is in boys.

As babies develop in the womb, the right side of the brain develops first and faster than the left side. No one really knows why this is, but it does mean that babies are more likely to respond to pattern, colour and shape, as the responses for these are mainly located in the right hemisphere. There has been a lot of discussion about whether the two hemispheres have different functions, but the latest view is that both sides of the brain are involved in most thinking processes, using the corpus callosum to communicate. The two halves in some ways reflect each other, but with one half taking the lead in orchestrating the process.

Right brain

One way these different lead roles has been described is that the right brain appears to be switched on by 'big picture' concepts and stimuli – colour, music, creativity, imagination, movement, space, dreams, art, processing meaning and often dealing with subconscious learning. This is the half of the brain that grows first and fastest, and that is why we provide early stimuli that feed the right side of the brain. Early years settings are visually exciting and offer hands-on activities, which appeal to children at this stage of brain development.

Left brain

The left side of the brain grows more slowly, particularly in boys, and helps the child to process the detail in their environment and experiences. The left hemisphere has a major role in speech and language development. It also handles the logical processing needed in spelling, grammar, order, sequence and pattern, helping children when they begin to learn about reading, writing and mathematics, particularly when it is written using letters and symbols.

So, as Max approaches his birth day, he already has the foundations for learning, and about 100 billion brain cells ready to respond. The growth in each region of his brain will depend on him receiving stimulation, which triggers activity in that region. This stimulation provides the foundation for learning.

What's special about brain cells?

There are several different sorts of brain cells, and they do different things. Neurons are the ones we talk about and know best, but some cells, called glia (or glial cells) are more numerous than neurons, and provide a support service in the brain. They clean up neurons, removing debris that affects smooth communication, they transport nutrients to neurons, provide the protective covering for links between them, help to regulate the spaces between neurons for optimum performance, and even digest any neurons that have died. There are somewhere between ten and 50 times more glia than neurons in our bodies, so why do we not hear much about these cells? Perhaps it's because their roles are not as interesting as neurons, as they organise and direct our movement, thinking, creativity and our very survival. However, without our glial cells our brains would not be able to function.

Each neuron in Max's brain is like a soft sea urchin, with the ability to grow tendrils all over it, waving in the amniotic fluid that fills the womb, searching for the chemicals and electrical messages that switch brain cells on. These tendrils, up to 200,000 on each neuron, are called dendrites, and the neuron will grow as many as it needs. Dendrites are very sensitive, reacting to the chemicals that find their way into Max's brain, and reaching out to link with other neurons, as they receive information from the rest of his body.

As well as all these dendrites, each neuron has a single thicker tendril, called the axon, which is responsible for transmitting information, including the information from the dendrites, to other neurons. Some of these axons are several feet long, the longest extends from the base of the spine to the big toe, and in an adult this can be as long as a metre! Each axon has a cluster of smaller filaments on the end, and this is where learning mainly takes place, as information is passed from synapse to synapse. Synapses form the junctions between neurons and a synapse's performance and shape changes when we learn something new.

The axon is much thicker and more complicated than the dendrites, and can have multiple terminals, enabling it to communicate with several dendrites at the same time. Clusters of these axons sometimes form cords or nerves, such as those in the spinal column. So, put simply, multiple dendrites on each neuron receive information, and the single axon on each neuron sends the information on to the next dendrite.

Repitition produces myelin

Many of the links between brain cells in Max's brain are still very 'soft', and are vulnerable until Max has had time to repeat the response or action many times. This repetition produces a fatty substance called myelin, which coats the soft links, protecting them, making them permanent and enabling faster responses to stimulation. Simple actions such as smiling, focusing on Angie's face, reaching out his hand, and every other thing Max ever learns or learns to do, will need concentrated practice to turn the soft wiring into hard wiring, making permanent structures in his brain and body, there for life.

The layers of myelin form in short sections all the way along each axon, with tiny gaps between each section, where the axon is exposed to the chemical rich fluid in the brain. These gaps have the rather romantic name of the Nodes of Ranvier, and as the axon produces electrical signals fed by the chemicals in the brain fluid, the myelin acts to speed up the passage of these electrical messages. In a well myelinated axon, the signal jumps from one node to the next 100 times faster than in non-myelinated axons.

As we practise and repeat actions some hard wiring will become so permanent that, by the time we are adults, we can do many things without thinking, recalling these sequences effortlessly and often unconsciously. Smiling, cleaning our teeth, putting on make-up, reading, swimming, riding a bike, or driving a car are all hard wired for many adults. We have done these things so many times that the links along a path of neurons have been permanently protected by a thick myelin sheath, and the trigger of picking up the toothbrush or turning the ignition key will start the sequence of movements, which then proceed smoothly and unconsciously. Arriving at work with no real memory of whether the last set of traffic-lights were red or green is a frightening example of this process. Myelin also allows us to recall experiences, both pleasant and unpleasant, so that a particular smell will bring back memories of a holiday or a piece of music may remind us of boring assembly times at school.

As Max repeats activities in the womb, even simple ones such as blinking and sucking, his body produces myelin too. These links, the ones that are used frequently, or that have a pleasurable response, will become hard-wired, permanent features of Max's brain at birth.

With all this activity, it's not surprising that babies need a lot of sleep. We all need sleep, because it is during sleep that our bodies have a chance to flush out the debris and toxins collected in our brains during waking time. We might all be more productive if we got enough sleep, and it is little wonder that children who do not have enough sleep find it difficult to engage with learning, and fail to remember what they learned the day before. Maybe we should add sleep clubs to breakfast and homework clubs, for those children who would benefit from a short sleep before embarking on the school day.

So, even in Max's unborn brain, and with added enthusiasm as he approaches full term, his axons are already sending and dendrites are already receiving information. However, the amount of activity in the brain is nothing like it will be once he is born. While he is in the womb, Max is starting to build the architecture of his brain; now, as he reaches full term, he will begin to use this architecture to help him think, and this needs much more than just linking brain cells.

Cells on the move

Brain cells start off identical to each other, but they move within the brain and take on different responsibilities almost from the moment of conception, so that by the time Max is born, his brain cells are all in the right places and have taken on their own roles, maintaining these roles for the rest of his life. Some will control movement, some will take in sights and sounds, yet others will manage memory and so on. At this stage, the parts of the brain that will enable Max to use language, to think, and to feel and manage emotions are not very well developed.

As his brain begins to function as a thinking human, he is producing thousands of neuron links and dendrites, far more than he really needs, responding to every stimulus, with no screening of information coming in. At this stage, every sensation is new, everything equally important, every stimulus needs its response. Later, during his first few years, he will 'prune' some of these, to make room for the information he really needs to keep, and those links that he does not need die back and cease to function.

Even at this young age, Max's brain is beginning to balance the influences of nature and nurture. His genes will direct the general layout and organisation of his brain, but the fine-tuning of his responses to the world outside, will be affected by the nurturing he receives. For instance, if he hears lots of language, and is lovingly handled, Max's brain will respond by growing more neuron links (or synapses) in his language-related brain areas. If Angie stops talking to him, and begins to handle him in a cold, dismissive way (perhaps as a result of post-natal depression) Max's brain will respond by pruning language synapses, or developing such weak links that they fall away from lack of use. His potential to become a confident communicator will be damaged.

Does it matter that Max is a boy?

Angie and Dale know that Max will be a boy, and they are happy about this. Dale loves football, and is really looking forward to sharing this interest with Max. Carly is lively and active, loves going to the park, and is interested in music and dancing, but she is not very sporty, she doesn't mind what the baby will be, she just wants a healthy baby! Judging by the kicks and elbowing from Max in the middle of the night, she thinks Dale might get his sports companion!

Max's sex was determined at the moment of conception, an event which has been likened to the throwing of a thousand dice, because every throw is different. If you threw these dice and photographed the resulting patterns and numbers, then threw the dice again, and again, and again, you would come up with a different result every time. It's the same with making babies – the genetic make-up of our DNA is so complex that, even with the same two parents, every conception is different, even in the case of identical twins.

One of the 'genetic dice' determines the sex of the baby, although, if you look at early embryos, there is no visible difference between the boys and the girls, as all embryos have genitalia like females. The difference only starts when the embryos destined to be boys start to produce testosterone at around the fourth month of pregnancy (that's why you have to wait until around the twentieth week for a scan that can tell you the sex of the baby with any certainty). Testosterone supports 'maleness', and has an effect on the body and the balance of brain, emphasising certain features, and turning the sexual organs from the default female to male. Testosterone levels are always higher in boys than girls, but girls do continue to produce small amounts of testosterone throughout their lives.

Testosterone test!

To find out the balance of testosterone in your body, do this simple experiment, which has been well researched. Put your right hand, palm down, on the table and look at the length of your fingers. Look at your second and fourth fingers (the ones on each side of your longest finger). In most men, the fourth finger is measurably longer than the second finger. In most women, these fingers are about the same length. I say 'most' – my fourth finger is quite a lot longer than my second and I am a woman with two children! The difference in your fingers indicates the level of testosterone in your body, with a bigger difference indicating more testosterone. Many males have lower testosterone levels, many females have higher testosterone levels.

This research is not just interesting for us as adults, but can help us to understand some of the differences between boys and girls. It seems that the higher the level of testosterone in the womb, the smaller the child's vocabulary may be at the age of two, as testosterone has been found to inhibit the parts of the brain that deal with language. Particularly high levels of testosterone in the womb may also affect the number of boys who attend clinics for speech and language delays, and are now thought to trigger Autism and Asperger's Syndrome, as the testosterone levels in some children appears to reduce the ability to recognise and respond to facial expressions and eye contact.

In the second trimester (between the third and sixth months of pregnancy) the amniotic fluid in the womb is flooded with testosterone that also triggers the genetic markers for both sex and gender: how masculine a boy, how feminine a girl the baby will be. This complex balance of sex and gender is a fascinating process, and we are all affected by our unique genetic make-up, which seems to place us on a gender spectrum, somewhere between the most masculine boy (resembling Rambo or The Hulk) and the most feminine girl (like Barbie or The Little Mermaid). It is also possible to end up at a different extreme, as a masculine girl who races to be first outside on the bikes or the swings, or a feminine boy who shows real tenderness for the dolls in the home corner. This is not an issue for early years practitioners, but cultural influences often work against children who have a less culturally acceptable balance of sex and gender. In the early years, practitioners and children are much more accepting of differences, recognising that the sex/gender balance results in a wide range of interests and personalities – not better or worse, just different. If Max ends up at the masculine end of the spectrum, he is likely to be heavier at birth, with more muscle, more red blood cells, and a tendency to enjoy active play.

Caring for boys and girls

Angie and Dale feel strongly that they should behave no differently with their new boy than they did with Carly, but they would be superhuman if they achieved this equality. It is very evident from research all over the world that adults react very differently to boys, even when they are babies. They touch, comfort, indulge, and particularly talk to boys and girls differently. Watch a loving dad with his baby girl, watch a nursery practitioner with a young boy, and you will see that adults are continuing to promote a situation where boys and girls are expected to behave and respond differently. And if you are still unsure, go into a baby clothing and equipment store – where everything for baby boys is blue, everything for baby girls is pink, young boys are expected to be active, demanding and adventurous, girls are expected to be pretty, loving and quiet. Even the logos on children's T-shirts underline this culture, with overwhelmingly pink and pastel 'Daddy's Princess' for girls, and bright blue or red 'Mud is Good' for boys. Birthday cards, children's comics, TV adverts all add to these cultural expectations of boys and girls, making it very difficult to unscramble the impact of:

- nature – our genetic make-up
- nurture – how we are raised by our parents
- culture – the pressures of the culture in which we live.

Just to complicate matters even further, Steven Pinker, a psychologist with an interest in thinking and language development, suggests that a fourth element of our make-up is the role of 'chance'. Our parents give us our nature in our genes, our family gives us our nurture, our community gives us our culture, but what about chance?

Think of the chances in your own lifetime – the teacher who sparked your interest in maths, the illness or accident which interrupted your schooling, the offer of a new job, the unexpected move due to a family breakdown or death. Many families are experiencing a whole range of chance events as a result of the recent expansion of the European Union, or the difficult economic times. Redundancy, debt, part-time working, families in poverty, later retirement, mobile families, and even the increase in grandparents looking after their grandchildren while both parents work, will all affect the current generation of children. A wide range of chances affect every child, and for Max, the chance of being a boy could be a blessing or a burden.

Sex and gender, and we need to consider both, are only two of the factors that will shape Max's body and brain, and much of that can already be predicted.

Genes or jeans?

We inherit half our genes from our mothers and half from our fathers, so Max's unique genetic code is partly inherited from Angie and her family, and partly from Dale and his family.

The HGP has helped us to find the genetic locations of many inherited diseases, and to confirm that some conditions such as Autism are linked to our genetic make-up. There are hundreds of conditions inherited through genes, and some of these are triggered by the unique combination of genes in each throw of the genetic dice.

Max has no history of inherited diseases, such as Down's Syndrome or Cystic Fibrosis, but many features, from his hair colour, eye colour, height and other physical characteristics result from a competition for dominance between his two sets of genes. Even in simple features, if one of his parents has a dominant trait, this will tend to over-ride the recessive trait from his other parent. Dominant traits include brown eyes, curly hair, dimples, freckles, or being double-jointed, and these would over-ride the influence of other traits such as blue eyes or straight hair. Mathematical, musical and artistic ability seem to be influenced by our genes. Angie loves singing, and has passed on this 'melody gene' to Carly, who sings constantly. Max may inherit this gene too.

Sporting ability seems to be genetically influenced too, although strength and stamina appear to be more heritable than balance or agility. Dale's interest in sport and his involvement in the local football team are likely to affect Max's interests as well as his abilities. So some of the influences on learning, and particularly the likes and dislikes Max will have in his life at home and at school, are already present in the womb, ready to be nurtured, and open to culture and chance.

Being a boy is a significant factor when we start to look at learning. We have already seen how, even in the womb, Max's brain and body are different from most girl embryos. He is likely to be heavier when he is born, with a bigger body and even a bigger brain. However, this does not necessarily give Max an advantage. As soon as he goes to school, the pressure will be on to achieve the skills that are seen as indicators of success, such as reading and writing, and here the girls seem to have a head start. We will return to this issue later.

It is now thought that although here are some real differences in the structure and development of the brains of boys and girls, the biggest difference is in how these brains are used. Small differences in chemicals and in the growth of different parts of the brain can result in big differences in behaviour and attitude.

For example, boys' bodies tend to contain much more testosterone, which increases aggression, competition, self-reliance and self-assertion. Girls' bodies tend to contain more oestrogen, which lowers aggression, competition, self-reliance and self-assertion. The Broca's and Wernicke's areas, which support speech and language are more highly active in girls, resulting in better verbal communication skills. The areas that deal with spatial relationships are more highly developed in boys' brains, resulting in a greater ability to understand and think about spatial relationships, such as geometry, map making and construction.

Summer or winter birth?

Max will be born in November, and this will be an advantage for him, particularly when he goes to school, as he will be nine months older than the youngest children in his class. Angie and Dale didn't plan it this way, and Carly is a summer born child, a factor that is noticeable to Angie when she takes her to nursery. Carly is smaller and less confident than the other children in her group, and Angie hopes this won't be a problem for her later.

Research now tells us that autumn born children are likely to be taller, more active and more confident than summer born children in the same year group, and that those two terms can make as much as 12% difference in their attainment at the end of their first year in school (the Reception year in England). However, unless it can be arranged for all babies to be born in September, the status quo is likely to remain, and we must rely on teachers and parents to use their skills to make sure that summer born children don't become stigmatised just for being younger.

As Max moves steadily and healthily towards his birth day, he seems to have a pretty good chance of succeeding in life and in learning.

The best start in life

How can Max make the best start in life? It's certainly not as simple as making sure he is born in the autumn! Making a successful child does start before birth, and some scientists would say that it starts before conception. The best chance for a healthy conception is for the mother and father to control their drinking, refrain from smoking and drugs, and eat healthily. Put simply, healthy parents produce healthy eggs and healthy sperm, and that has the best chance of resulting in a healthy baby.

During pregnancy, all mothers should continue to restrict their drinking, eat healthily, and balance exercise with plenty of rest. If they want their baby to have a really good start, they will talk and sing to them, make contact by stroking their own skin, keep noise and violent movement to a minimum, and reduce family stress.

Defining the optimum environment for learning is easily described, but more difficult for a busy mother to achieve. Angie needs to eat well, rest a lot, keep the environment quiet and positive, and talk to her baby as if she can really see him! Her diet will affect his food choices for the rest of his life, and what she drinks will be what her baby drinks. Fortunately babies don't need clothes or toys in the womb, but they are able to hear human voices and other sounds, they can sense stress and tiredness even though they cannot name them, and they rely on their mother to keep them safe. They will never again need so little financial support, but they will never again be so vulnerable.

Dale and Angie need to spend time together, and with Carly – once Max is born, there won't be much time for this.

A message from Max

I am not just a collection of motionless cells, waiting for the moment of birth to start growing and changing. My body and brain began to grow and learn from the moment of conception, and as soon as my brain began to develop, I began to be influenced by messages from the outside world. I am like my mother and my father, a unique mixture, different from my sister, and not just in the obvious ways that you can see. My unique nature will also be changed by every experience you provide for me. I can already hear and feel messages from the outside world through my mother's body and through the fluid that surrounds me. These sounds, tastes feelings and emotions will influence me for the rest of my life.

You can make a real difference to my future by the way you behave during the time I am in the womb as well as during the years to come.

Practitioners

- Do everything you can to help parents understand that learning starts before birth. A good time to talk about babies is before they are born, not after.

- Educating parents about very early learning is an investment that will pay off when children come to nursery or school. Encourage parents to talk and sing to their babies in the womb, as this will create the architecture for language.

- Be aware of children who are born in the summer months, they may develop noticeably more slowly than autumn born children, and are always the youngest in their year group.

- Diet, smoking, sleep and alcohol all have a profound effect on brain growth. Practitioners and teachers have a duty to help parents make wise choices at this crucial stage.

Parents

- Think about the tension between nature, nurture, culture and chance. Learning is a complex process, affected by family characteristics and genetic make-up.

- Boys and girls really are different, developing in different ways and at different rates. We should treat all children as individuals.

- How you behave, what you eat and drink and even the tone of your voice will have an effect on your unborn child. Your baby really is what you eat, influenced by such things as your tastes in food, the quality of your diet, and the amount of sleep and exercise you take. Try to limit alcohol and smoking during pregnancy.

- Your baby can hear you! Make sure what they hear keeps them calm and stress free. During pregnancy, your stress levels will be carried in the amniotic fluid to your child.

Interlude 1 Nature, nurture, culture and a life of chances: the latest discussions

'All our behaviours are a result of neurophysiological activity in the brain. There is no reason to believe there is any magic going on.'

Steven Pinker; cognitive scientist

If we accept this, that there is no magic going on, how are these neurophysiological activities affected by our own unique make-up? In Max's story I discussed some of the factors that influence each of us and make us the people we are. In the first of several interludes throughout this book, I'd like to look more closely at some of the factors that affect children's ability to learn and succeed in school. In this one, I examine more closely the relationship between nature, nurture, culture and chance.

Nature

The effect of nature on each of us is becoming clearer every day, as the work of the HGP really starts to have an impact. We can already identify and locate many of the talents and disadvantages in our individual genomes, including tendencies to inherited diseases, and soon we will be able to 'switch off' some of these problems, or 'switch on' additional talents. At the very least it will help doctors to prescribe treatments that are closely targeted to our individual needs, with the potential to increase the number of recoveries from previously fatal or disabling conditions. For instance, it is now possible to find out whether a remaining twin is likely to die from the same illness, or commit the same crimes as their sibling.

As time goes on, the part played by our genes becomes even more complex as so many families separate and recombine during our lives, with new family groupings and relationships complicating the genetic pattern.

Nurture

Any discussion of the part played by nurture or upbringing is also problematic. The simple cause and effect of family relationships experienced even a century ago has gone forever. We all know so much about what other people do, and we have so much advice on how we should be bringing up our children, so many tips for managing behaviour, feeding our family on a budget, boosting our children's test scores, improving our relationships, locating and exploiting their talents and eliminating their problems, that anyone would think we need do no more than follow this advice. Available at the touch of a finger, on line, on our phones, on social networks, on TV and in books, magazines and newspapers, this endless guidance bedazzles and confuses us all, particularly young and worried parents who in the past would have used local support systems of parents and grandparents in bringing up their children.

Of course, there are plenty of people in the public eye who say 'All we need to do to solve cultural problems is to reintroduce smacking, learning by rote, national service, longer skirts, or cold baths'. It is easy to say, 'It never did me any harm!' and indeed I was lucky to be brought up by caring parents in a stable family where I was protected, encouraged, nurtured and inspired to be the best I could be. But, despite the open fields, muddy shores and grazed knees of my childhood days, I would not wish the noisy and painful dental care, the meaningless rote learning of my schooling, the cold bedrooms, bland post-war food and limited horizons of my childhood on any child now. We can't turn the clock back even if we could agree when it should stop.

Progress will come, and we have to accept that with progress comes a need for us to exercise our own will as adults and teach our children to do so too. Endless choice does not mean we have to have everything, free access to social networking comes with its own horror stories that we must either accept or work to change. Adults need to stop trying just to be their children's friends. They must take responsibility for their own actions, helping their children to cope with the ever-faster pace of life, and the pressures it brings.

What children need is what they have always needed: nurturing that makes them feel secure yet adventurous, able to take advantage of all the wonderful opportunities available to them, and with the personal, social and educational skills they need to succeed whatever adult life brings their way. Work is no longer the driver for getting qualifications, so we need to nurture a desire to learn, and an interest in everything, along with the ability to see the risks and dangers associated with a fast moving world. The job of bringing up our children has never been harder, and it is a job for all of us, not just parents.

Culture

Part of that responsibility for each of us is to do what we can to reduce the negative effects of our culture on the next generation. We frequently hear, 'Someone should do something about that!' with little indication of who that 'someone' should be. We have all been part of constructing a culture that preaches equality, but accepts a widening gap between the rich and the poor, sometimes described as the hourglass of inequality, with the two ends of society becoming separated by a reducing number of people in the middle.

The whole of society, led by a caring government, now need to do what it can to reduce the number of children being brought up in poverty, and to give the current generation of children a real opportunity to become agents of change, building a future where the 'grab it while you can' culture is replaced by something more positive.

Chance

In a government document on the early years curriculum, ten 'chance elements' are identified as key factors in success at school. They play a vital part in children's futures, and for some the combination is a recipe for failure. They are:

- Ethnicity (the ethnic heritage of the child and their family)
- Parent education (educated parents produce successful children)
- Home language or mother tongue
- Family income (for all the extras)
- Socio-economic status of the family (where the family is in the local and national 'pecking order')

- Gender (I think they mean sex!)
- Parental involvement in school activities (not 'helicopter parenting', but genuine interest and support)
- The quality of pre-school experience (high quality pre-school experiences have been proven to have a lasting effect)
- Home learning environment (not homework, but an environment where a child can play alone or with friends, be quiet, relax, read, work on a computer, talk to their family)
- Month of birth (summer born children are vulnerable)

The effect of each of these key characteristics is there for each child, many of them present from the day of birth and none of them in a child's control. Our world, and the world of every child, is governed by chance, and we are all subject to chances every day, some of which will change our lives – making predictions about individuals complex and pretty impossible to predict.

What if?

Ask yourself these 'What if?' questions:

- What if I was brought up by my grandparents, not my parents?
- What if I had three more siblings than I have?
- What if I hadn't met my current partner?
- What if that near-miss when I walked off the pavement without looking had resulted in a broken back and life in a wheelchair?
- What if I won the lottery?
- What if I had been born the other sex, and 20 cm taller or shorter than I am, or had different colour hair or skin?
- What if I had decided on a different job or career?
- What if one of my teachers had unlocked in me a talent for maths, painting or music?

These 'what-ifs' are called counterfactuals, alternative scenarios of our own lives, and they are worth thinking about, as they make us realise how our lives are governed by so much more than our genetic make-up, our upbringing and the culture we live in.

Jenny's journey

Here's an example of the chances experienced by Jenny before her eighth birthday. Chance made just as much difference to her future as those counterfactual options could to you:

- After she is born, and despite advice from the Health Visitor, her parents decide not to immunize her against measles, mumps and rubella.
- The family moves to live in a house with access for Jenny and her friends to go out of the back garden into fields and a wood.
- At three, she catches measles, and on recovery she develops a squint and has to have treatment resulting in wearing glasses, for which she is teased at school.
- At four years of age a boy moves in next door, who will be Jenny's best friend for the rest of her life.
- Due to staff illness, she has four different teachers during her first year in school.
- When she is seven, Jenny's mum wins a modest prize in the National Lottery. This is big enough for her to splash out on holidays and toys for the children, but it soon runs out, and she has overspent, resulting in yet another house move, this time to a small flat in a tower block.

Such simple chances can have a profound effect on Jenny's life. Children who are not immunised are at risk of permanent side-effects from the diseases they may catch. Knowing and feeling secure in the people she meets outside her home, and particularly her first encounters in school, may influence Jenny's learning for the rest of her life. Where you live, whether this is somewhere with green space, or a tower block can again affect your life. Children who grow up with plenty of outdoor experience and sunshine, experience less stress and are generally calmer. The final counterfactual, which we all consider even if we never buy a ticket, of winning the Lottery, can be an opportunity or a disaster.

This element of chance in our lives, combined with the culture in which we are brought up, may account for as much as half of the influence on what we become.

'Statisticians tell us that people underestimate the sheer number of coincidences that are bound to happen in a world governed by chance.'

Steven Pinker

Recent developments

During the writing of this book, the nature/nurture debate has taken another turn, which caused a ripple in the fabric of the education and parenting universe. It was triggered by two events – the first was the publication of a book by Kathryn Asbury (University of York), and Robert Plomin (Professor of Behavioural Genetics at King's College London). *G is for Genes* (2013, John Wiley & Sons) is a layman's guide to research into the differences in attainment in exams at 16. The authors are neuroscientists, who have examined the link between genetic make-up and exam results at 16, using information on a large group of twins, the TEDS (Twins' Early Development Study). The 'headline' outcome of this piece of research is the finding that over 50% of the difference between the highest and lowest scores in GCSE (General Certificate of Education) could be assigned to genetic influences.

The second 'stone in the gene pool' was a paper written by Dominic Cummings, a senior education policy consultant at the time. This dense and complex paper covers a wide range of topics, including the suggestion that governments might profitably look at how to respond to the TEDS research and consider an education system influenced by the research into genetic factors. He appears to imply that, in the future, we may see schools where children's genomes will define their educational programme.

Two questions follow:

- Are we seeing the emergence of eugenics by the back door (survival of the fittest and improvement of the human race by enabling only the most able to succeed)?
- Or is this a sensible and sensitive suggestion for differentiating school provision by using each child's genetic profile to ensure they get the best-matched provision possible?

Your start in life

We all know that parents with high intelligence themselves, and an interest in ideas and in problem solving, who read books and talk to their children, will produce children who are like them, likely to do better at school and in life. It's not the books that make the children better learners – it's the genes!

When children are born into families where money is scarce, parents have had a less successful education themselves, nutrition is poor, TV is purely entertainment, and value for schools and learning is low, they will not do as well.

What Plomin's research on about 6,500 pairs of twins born in England and Wales appears to tell us is that at the age of 16, more than 50% of the difference between the top and bottom results in GCSE is down to heredity, the genes children receive from their parents at the moment of conception. Plomin also says that environmental influences from home and school make around 30% of the difference. Should we be surprised at this? Should we all give up parenting and teaching? And how do we affect the remaining 20% of potential not mentioned in Plomin's paper?

We know that children whose parents are interested in them, whose mothers have had a good education themselves, and particularly those who have high aspirations for their children will do better. A teacher knows this almost from the moment the child walks through the door of their classroom or setting. They can also pick up which children will be slower to learn, or will struggle to concentrate. These children will not have had the benefit of a good diet or enough sleep, have no books at home, not enough talk, too much screen time, and probably parents who did not enjoy or do well at school themselves. Again it's not the lack of books that is the problem, it's the long line of deprived lives standing behind each child.

When I met the shortlisted candidates for deputy headship of the school where I was head, a school in a deprived area in the Midlands of England, one said, 'The children here are so small. They are much smaller than the children in my present school. Why are they so small?'

I could have answered in several ways. 'It may be because almost all the children in this school come from families living on benefit; or because most of the mothers smoke, and many drink heavily, even during pregnancy; or because there are no shops on the estate as they are always ransacked; or because a large proportion of children are raised by lone parents; or because the only meal many of them have during the day is a free school meal; or because the only reason for anyone in the family to get up is to bring them to school.' Or I could have said, 'It's just all in their genes, poor parents produce poor children, and there's nothing we can do to change it.' However, what I did say was that we took each child as an individual and looked past this inheritance of poverty into a better future.

The influence of school

Robert Plomin and Dominic Cummings both say that we should look carefully at the 'in-school' factors that affect attainment, and of these, children's genetic make-up may account for up to 80% of the *difference* between the highest exam or test score and the lowest in any school, whether this is from the phonics screening at the age of five or six, or reading tests at ages seven or 11.

For some time, the teaching profession has been pleading for a method that takes into account the local circumstances within a school that affect overall attainment levels. They would welcome any method that encourages teachers to look more closely at children's needs, and schools to feel that the 'value' they add is recognised, instead of the current fixation on results and trying to make every child and every school the same.

What we all need to remember is that we have always tried to make the difference within the other 20% of potential, so every child can become the best they can be. Teachers and parents all do this by using a massive toolbox of techniques, including individual support, differentiated tasks, different teaching and learning styles, working closely between school and home, involving outside agencies, and above all, telling every child every day that they matter to us and we believe in them, whatever their genetic make-up. There are hundreds and thousands of adults alive today who would not be doing what they are doing now if it wasn't for a dedicated teacher or other adult who looked for the 20% and never let genetics get in the way of giving a child the chance to excel in something that their genetic profile might never suggest as suitable for them.

Active model of education

So what would a 'gene school' (not a gene pool) look like? In the first eugenics panic, newspaper articles implied that every decision on provision would be made through a simple combination of regular tests and genetic screening, implying that there would be no room for the human element, the bit that makes teachers different from teaching machines. However, in the digest of the original paper, author Robert Plomin says something different:

'Rather than a passive model of schooling as instruction (instruere, 'to build in'), we propose an active model of education (educare, 'to bring out') in which children create their own educational experiences in part on the basis of their genetic propensities, which supports the trend towards personalised learning.'

Such schools would engage in 'active genotype-environment correlation', which occurs when:

'... children select, modify, and construct or re-construct experiences that are correlated with their genetic propensities. For example, children who like to read can cultivate their own reading in the library, on the internet, and via friends.'

Genetic influence on educational achievement Robert Plomin et al

This is a very different school from the one that pops up when we talk about eugenics and streaming according to external exams. Plomin also suggests that there is less genetic influence in appetite than in aptitude, implying that the 'will' may be just as important as the 'skill'. A thirst for knowledge may be genetically manufactured, but without the appetite for learning, the child may not be able to make best use of this genetic aptitude.

Is this not where the skilled teacher comes in? Is this not what I see and hear many teachers trying to do? Following the interests and aptitudes of the children in their class at the moment, not planning a 'programme' without reference to these. If schools could be allowed to modify the curriculum to fit the child, rather than trying to force the to child fit the curriculum, we might have a hope of 'genetically modifying' schools to meet the needs of the child.

In his paper, *Genetic influence on educational achievement*, Robert Plomin and his co-researchers conclude with the following:

'In closing, we note that accepting the evidence for strong genetic influence on individual differences in educational achievement has no necessary implications for educational policy, because policy depends on values as well as knowledge. For example, a deep-seated fear is that accepting the importance of genetics justifies inequities – educating the best and forgetting the rest. However, depending on one's values, the opposite position could be taken, such as putting

more educational resources into the lower end of the distribution to guarantee that all children reach minimal standards of literacy and numeracy, so that they are not excluded from our increasingly technological societies. It is to be hoped that better policy decisions will be made with knowledge than without. Part of that knowledge is the strong genetic contribution to individual differences in educational achievement.'

So it is clear, nature, nurture, culture and chance, combine to be major influences on lives, and are also the influences on learning. The future in education will be interesting, as politicians, teachers and parents struggle to find agreement on a new way of working, or worse, ignore the evidence and continue to emphasise sameness, a pale shadow of equality.

Points to ponder

- If nature (our genetic make-up) is so important, how could we use additional information about individual children's genetic features and 'heritable' characteristics to help us to understand how they learn, and the difficulties, disabilities and delays they might have?

- How can individuals influence education policy and practice in settings and schools take a more holistic view of nature, nurture, culture <u>and</u> chance, particularly if there is a pressure to make decisions purely based on children's innate abilities (just their nature)?

- In the research quoted in this interlude, there is a suggestion that nature, nurture and culture may combine to account for 80% of the difference between the highest and lowest achievers. What would be the features of a setting or school that promotes 'educare' and personalised learning – taking into account every child's individual nature? Are there already schools where this method is already in place? What would be the problems in setting up such individually based provision?

Stage 2 After the beginning – Mari is eight months old

'A child is born with the potential ability to learn Chinese or Swahili, play a kazoo, climb a tree, make a strudel or a birdhouse, take pleasure in finding the coordinates of a star. Genetic inheritance determines a child's abilities and weaknesses. But those who raise a child call forth from that matrix the traits and talents they consider important.'

Emilie Buchwald, writer

Let's move on and look at life after birth, the period when brain cells are at their most active, when the world has everything to offer. The temporary shock of birth is over, the world is a wonderful place to be, and even your own fingers or feet, or the sunshine reflecting off the mobile over your cot can delight you. Here is Mari, she is eight months old:

Mari is lying in her cot. It's very early in the morning and she has woken up before her mum. However, she doesn't cry, she lies awake, looking round her at her room and doing some leg stretching exercises that might look to us like random kicking. Sometimes she reaches out and catches her feet, pulling them to her mouth. At this stage babies will always try to put things in their mouths, it's because there are more sensory nerve endings in their tongues and the insides of their mouths than in their hands, so they get more information about objects this way. We only learn much later that putting everything in our mouths is neither polite nor always possible!

Above Mari's cot is a mobile, turning gently, and just out of reach enough to encourage her to reach up for the small soft toys hanging there. Sometimes she can catch one of them, but her grip is not yet secure enough to hold on for long. The mobile isn't a musical, light-flashing one, just a simple selection of soft animals in bright colours, and Mari isn't only practising her reaching and holding, she is practising looking and focusing on a moving object, following the animals as they pass through her field of vision. As she watches, her hands are running up and down the bars of her cot, feeling the texture of the wood. Babies at this stage need to touch everything in their reach, experiencing with touch, taste and sound, as well as sight. Everything is new, everything is there to learn, and she absorbs everything.

Mari's nightlight has a revolving shade, throwing coloured shapes over the ceiling, and in her cot there are some small board books, and two of her favourite toys of the moment –

a green teddy and another animal, which defies description, but makes Mari smile every time she sees it. Mari's room, although simply equipped, is exactly suited to her needs. She doesn't need too much stimulation, as this will make her wake too quickly and encourage over-stimulated activity such as shouting and bouncing. What she needs is a quiet, calm waking, with familiar objects and something to watch.

Mari's mum wakes up. Mari can hear her and the kicking gets even more excited. She pulls herself up on the cot bars and stands, secure, if a bit wobbly, and starts to vocalise, gurgling, squealing and waving her arms expectantly. Of course at this stage she can't wave and hold on at the same time, so she sits down abruptly, laughing as her mum appears round the door.

Mari's family

Eugenia is mostly raising Mari by herself. Her partner, Jason, drives a truck, travelling every week from England to Spain and back, so he is only at home for a few days at a time, but he keeps in touch regularly by mobile, and as Eugenia's family live in Spain, she gets news of them when he comes near their village on his driving journeys.

When he is at home, Jason is a very attentive and conscientious parent. He loves his little daughter, and wants to give her the best start in life, but his hopes as a boy that the streets would be paved with gold if he could only get to England have been dashed by reality, and he has to get work where he can. Eugenia is on unpaid leave from her job as a care assistant in a residential home. She is hoping they will take her back when Mari is old enough to go to nursery. Money is a problem, but both parents are committed to making sure that Mari gets what she needs.

Like most meals with Mari, breakfast is a companionable but pretty messy event. Eugenia encourages Mari to feed herself with dry cereal, fruit and toast, but she still has formula milk from a bottle. Mari breastfed her until recently, knowing that the benefits of breastfeeding are many, not just in nutrition, but in the close contact and physical nurturing it provides.

Even though she hasn't done much reading about parenting, Eugenia remembers a lot from her own childhood. She is the oldest of six children, and was drawn into the role of extra mum for the youngest of her brothers and sisters. She knows that young children need plenty of love, simple toys, good food and space out of doors to play. She tries to provide these for Mari.

Today it's the Baby Club session at the community centre. Mari and Eugenia love this, as it gives them both a chance to meet other people, and there is a garden there, with a lawn, lots of toys for the children, and seats for the parents where they can sit and chat. Eugenia's English is improving all the time, and she is thinking about going for some extra English lessons at the centre, as they have a crèche and she is happier about leaving Mari now she is a bit older. Last week the community leaders at the Baby Club invited someone to come and demonstrate baby massage, which Eugenia has tried at home, although Mari is very wriggly and she wished they had started massage when she was much younger!

This week the Baby Club workers are offering some help with making treasure baskets, collections of everyday objects for babies who can sit unsupported to play with. Eugenia knows that children love familiar objects and would often prefer to have the contents of a kitchen cupboard to play with than any shop-bought toy. She watches and listens carefully and decides that when Mari is having her nap, she will begin to collect some things to start a treasure basket for her. One of the first things she will put in is a small photo frame with a picture of Mari's grandparents and cousins in Spain.

On the way home they call in at the care home where Eugenia worked before Mari was born. The elderly residents there love to see her and the baby, and even some of the more withdrawn residents will come out of their shells when Mari visits. The care home is next to the market, so they walk through it as they go home for lunch. Mari points and waves at the strawberries, her current favourite fruit, and they bring some home for a treat. Mari is at the stage when pointing is a feature, and she points at everything. Eugenia sometimes thinks Mari just wants everything she points at, but Mari is on the very edge of beginning to talk and the pointing indicates she wants to know what something is called.

Back at home, after lunch and a short nap, Mari and Eugenia play together with simple toys and first books. Eugenia begins to look for things to put in the treasure basket, starting with the little photo frame, a wooden spoon, keys on a string, a little metal bowl, a sponge, a shell, a toothbrush, a real lemon, an old purse, a string of beads and a little gift box. She will add to these as she finds other objects that she thinks Mari will like. The treasure basket has to be kept in a big plastic bowl for now, but when Jason rings her, Eugenia will ask him to bring a round Spanish basket when he comes home next. Her mum will show him where to get one.

How is Mari doing?

Eugenia could look up some developmental milestones on the internet, which will tell her broadly what she should expect Mari to be able to do. However, these milestones should come with a warning that parents should not use them as a strict measure of either their child's development, or their parenting abilities. Eugenia has a lot of experience of growing children, and she doesn't want or need to be distracted by checklists. She knows that Mari is healthy and happy, growing well and beginning to show some of the features of an emerging toddler.

Attachment at home

The most important area of development in the first 12 months is in what experts call attachment. When humans lived in prehistoric times, and in more dangerous times since, they developed a vital survival instinct, to ensure that babies and young children didn't wander away from their parents and into danger. This instinct is the attachment instinct, and young children still have it, like an invisible string between them and their mother.

The adult provides safety, but also provides a model for behaviour and relationships as well as a secure base, and attachment provides much of the foundation for the child's future personal development. Every baby needs to feel attached to at least one person, and ideally more than one. This collection of key people usually starts with the child's mother, but will include their other parent, and might include a grandparent, a nursery worker, a neighbour, childminder, anyone who the child feels able to return to in times of need and know they will be there. These key adults need to feel the attachment too, and when they do, they try hard to 'tune in' to what the child needs and is feeling, and make sure they provide the secure base from which she or he can explore.

Mari has that secure attachment with Eugenia, but circumstances mean that her attachment to Jason is less secure as she is not old enough to understand why sometimes he is available, and sometimes he is not.

The deep relationship of attachment (some people call this relationship bonding) began when Mari was in the womb, and has become deeper since, especially because Jason is away so much. Mari is now going through the stage where she becomes distressed when Eugenia has to leave her, even to go to the bathroom, and although this is a quite natural part of attachment, both sides are equally affected. In Mari's case, as in the cases of many children brought up by a lone parent, the bond with a single adult may be very deep, and can make starting nursery or school more difficult.

Attachment at nursery

When Mari attends a nursery or pre-school, a key person from the nursery staff will be named as the secure base and safe haven for her during the time when Eugenia can't be present. This relationship may become even more important for Mari than for a child with attachment to a wider range of adults.

It is now very evident that children with less secure attachments to adults have higher levels of stress chemicals in their bodies, and find it more difficult to adapt to new circumstances or take advantage of the activities and experiences offered in nursery or pre-school. The stress chemicals inhibit their learning, and the effect on their personal development may well be permanent.

Baby massage is one way to increase attachment, although, as they seem to have a really strong bond, Mari and Eugenia don't really need help here. Massage reduces stress in mothers and babies, and is often a way to help anxious mothers to touch and handle their babies more. So called 'skin to skin' contact is now thought to be a very good stimulant for babies' bodies and brains, not just straight after their birth, but during the months before they learn to crawl.

When adults are attached to a child in a sensitive way that does not restrict the child's freedom to develop; the adult becomes attuned to the child's needs, and tries to respond to these. Attunement is a process where the adult watches and listens very carefully to the child, so they know them very well, and can respond to their needs, help them to widen their group of contacts, and learn to feel comfortable with themselves. Eugenia is thinking about Mari's needs as well as her own as she considers using a crèche to enable her to go to English classes.

Mari and learning

Mari's emotional and social development is crucial to learning. Children with secure attachments and a confident, positive approach to life will be ready to learn at home, in the community and in any early years setting they attend. However, learning is not just about personal development, vital though that is. Children need to be able to communicate with others through words and gestures, and manage their bodies as well as their feelings. The development of language and physical skills is intertwined with the management of feelings and relationships.

Learning language

In language development Mari is progressing well. She obviously has control of her mouth and lips, and this will certainly have been helped by eating a wide range of finger foods, and things that need squishing and chewing with her emerging teeth. Children who have been weaned very late, or do not experience 'lumpy' foods, are often late or indistinct talkers, and the use of dummies or comforters can also inhibit talking. Eating and talking are closely linked, so parents and practitioners would be well advised to wean children away from foods without lumps, as we are producing a generation of children who won't eat any food with 'bits' in. The debate about early weaning is covered later in this book.

Eugenia has spent a huge amount of time with Mari since she was born, and during this time, she has spoken and sung to her in Spanish, her own native language. Like most parents, she naturally uses a higher, sing-song voice, movements and exaggerated expressions as she speaks, all of which babies love. She also has 'conversations' with Mari, waiting for Mari to respond to comments, questions and the beginnings of songs with sounds or expressions, and praising these when they come. These behaviours will all help to stimulate the parts of Mari's brain that are engaged with language. Of course, the language receptors in her brain will respond more readily to Spanish, but this isn't a problem, Mari will adjust very easily to learning English if she goes to the crèche. She is sociable, and is at an ideal age for learning an additional language.

Mari already loves the nursery songs and finger rhymes her mum uses, but Eugenia is worried that she should have been teaching Mari in English. As Mari starts to talk, Eugenia is committed to taking her to any place where she will hear and learn English, and to learn more English herself. She has made friends with another mum at the Baby Group, and they visit each other's homes every week for a coffee and chat. This, and the crèche should help Mari to get used to other people.

Children who are raised in bilingual homes do not seem to be disadvantaged as long as they learn both languages at an early stage, while their brains are 'plastic'. Research concludes that bilingual children usually do better at school, particularly in reading, so Eugenia has two tasks. The first is to continue to continue to speak Spanish herself, and the second is to expose Mari to English as much as she can.

At eight months Mari has a wide range of communication tools – sounds, expressions and gestures at her command, and she can and often does point at things she wants, or wants Eugenia to name for her. She also has a few words, or approximate words such as 'da', used indiscriminately for Jason and any other men she sees; 'mamamam' means either hurry up with my food, or Mum; 'baba' is baby or any other small child (often older than her); 'nana' is banana. There are some other words that she is approximating, but they are not yet really in her vocabulary.

At this age, Mari can understand many more words than she can say, and this will be the case until she is an adult. She is on the threshold of language explosion; she has all the sounds and some of the meanings, and before long she will begin to collect hundreds of words a week. By the time Mari is six, she will have an expressive vocabulary of 2,600 words she can say, and a receptive vocabulary of 20,000–24,000 words she understands.

Learning to move

Mari's physical development is also well within the normal range. She loves swinging, spinning and rocking – all very good for brain development as they agitate the fluid in the inner ear, making hearing more acute and helping with focus and attention. Mari loves being swung by her dad and as soon as he appears she puts up her arms to him. When Jason is away, Eugenia takes Mari to the park and they enjoy baby swings, bouncy horses and the roundabout. In areas where swings have been removed for safety reasons, children and their parents are deprived of these simple, enjoyable activities, which also stimulate the brain.

Although Mari shows no sign of crawling, there is no need for Eugenia to worry. Many children move straight from rolling and sitting to standing, without crawling at all, and Mari may be one of these. She is just beginning to pull herself to standing, using low furniture or the bars of her cot, and will probably begin to 'cruise' round the furniture very soon. Then Eugenia will discover the delights and perils of living with a mobile baby. Most children walk at around their first birthday, and Mari will probably do this too. The muscles of the body develop in a specific sequence in all babies and young children:

- The first movement muscles to develop are called the core muscles, in the back, trunk and neck, enabling babies to lift and turn their heads, and to arch their spines in preparation for turning over. Once a baby can control their back and stomach muscles, they can sit, first propped on a cushion, then independently.

- Development then moves out from the body and down the limbs, and you will often see babies doing 'workouts' of these limb muscles as they lie in their cots or on playmats, waving to exercise their shoulders and arms, kicking to exercise their hips, legs and feet. As soon as babies can turn their bodies over and roll, they can begin to use these leg and arm muscles, doing press-ups as they lift their heads and shoulders resting on their elbows or hands, drawing their knees under them to raise their trunks on four wobbly supports. They often stay in this 'bridge' position, as if puzzled about what to do next, until they collapse to the floor again.

- Some babies never go through the crawling stage, they just sit or lie until they embark on the standing or 'cruising' stage, working on their thigh, arm and ankle muscles, which they use to heave themselves to their feet. At first, standing is also an unpredictable activity and babies often find themselves sitting down suddenly, as the complex arrangement of muscles suddenly fails. However, one attribute that all human babies have is persistence, and the combination of praise and a new outlook keep them going.

- They repeat the standing activity again, and again and again until at last they have myelinated the control of muscles in their bodies, balancing and grabbing to help the standing skill, and can start to move sideways to go cruising around the furniture. Just think what an achievement that is – controlling head, body, shoulders, legs, hands and feet in the interests of standing on two feet!

- Cruising is often a short stage, as the thrill of moving about takes over, and one day, given the enthusiasm of their parents and carers, they take that first step unaided, usually to reach a favourite person or a toy.

In short, muscle development progresses from the core of the body to the extremities, from the body down to the feet and out to the hands. Fine motor muscles, particularly those of the hands and fingers, are among the last to develop, which is why some children, and particularly some boys do not gain full control of their hands and fingers until they are three, four or even five years old. The late blooming of these fine motor muscles in some children often results in concern among parents and practitioners which has been intensified by the current emphasis on writing at an inappropriately early age.

Mari has learned to sit unaided and is beginning to pull herself upright, she can reach and grasp objects, move objects from one hand to another, and, importantly, let go of them again. The muscles for letting go, and the instructions from her brain to do so, develop later than those for grasping, which is why babies sometimes get hold of adults' hair or glasses and don't know how to let go. Eugenia makes sure Mari has plenty of practice as she gives her small finger foods at every meal, and Eugenia's childhood in Spain is still evident in the types of food she provides for Mari and herself. As a lone parent, she is more likely to share mealtimes with her child, and Mari eats much the same things as her mother does, just cut up smaller. In this way she develops a taste for a wide range of vegetables, rice, pasta and seasonings.

Fine motor skills, those that Mari will eventually need to learn to read and write, are also developing well. Her eyes are functioning together, seeing objects clearly as she focuses both at close and more distant range. Her fingers and hands are becoming more coordinated, so she can isolate her index finger to poke and point, and pick up small objects with a 'pincer grip'.

Because Mari can now sit unaided, and needs lots of practice in exploring things, this is the ideal time to offer a treasure basket, so the advice from the Baby Group is timely. Treasure baskets are collections of familiar objects, ideally of natural materials – wood, metal, fabric, paper and card, along with pebbles, shells, fir cones and big seeds, offered to babies in a basket that they can sit by and reach into.

Learning to play

Children at Mari's stage of development need to be able to reach and grasp the objects that interest them, but because they haven't yet learned the words to ask for the things they want, frustration sometimes leads to grizzling and irritation. Parents try to guess what their babies want, but often the frustration just spreads from baby to mother as things are offered and rejected. The treasure basket offers a range of interesting objects, within reach, and where the baby can choose what interests them. Eleanor Goldschmeid, who first thought of the idea, had watched how babies love to explore their mums' handbags or the contents of drawers, boxes and cupboards, and developed this idea into a valuable explorative experience for babies which avoids dribble on their mum's phone, or the danger of swallowing small objects not really intended for baby play.

A treasure basket is thought by many experts in early learning to be one of the best 'learning toys' that a parent or practitioner can provide, and they are now found in many nurseries and daycare settings. As well as being easily assembled and reasonably cheap, the range of objects gives the child some of the earliest opportunities to choose, to manipulate objects, and to experience a range of textures, colours and shapes. People who watch babies with treasure baskets say that the levels of concentration observed are quite unusual for children of this age, and some babies have been seen playing with a basket for up to an hour, without the support of an adult. Of course, Eugenia should not and will not use a treasure basket as a reason for leaving Mari alone, but she will make sure she stays in view, doing something else while Mari plays.

Those vital first months outside the womb

There is often a view that very young babies have few demands and only need to be warm, fed and changed. This is certainly untrue. We now know that how a baby is treated in the first months after birth is vitally important, not just for childhood but for life. Which of the babies described below do you think will thrive?

- Baby 1 has all-day care at home, with a non-English speaking untrained 'nanny', who has recently arrived in the UK. She spends most of her time on her mobile phone to her friends, or watching TV. The employer insists that the baby should be taken to the park every day, but the nanny just walks to the park, sits on a bench and continues her phoning and texting.

- Baby 2 attends a city nursery where rows of cots fill the room. The room is clean and warm, and the babies are fed regularly, and when they are awake, they each have a bouncy chair to sit in, which they also sit in to be fed. The practitioners are under pressure to deal with so many babies, and the nursery employs very young (and cheap) carers, who have had little training or understanding of child development. There is very little one-to-one time or stimulation, and the only time the babies are touched is when they are changed, or moved from cot to bouncy chair and back. Information is logged about how much formula each child has drunk, and how often they have had a nappy change, and parents have an update on these activities every day. This nursery is so busy that there is no time for attachment or attunement with individual babies, and the 'key person' duties are restricted to record keeping and paperwork.

- Baby 3 attends a nursery where there is an experienced nursery practitioner for every two babies. This practitioner is named and well known to the family, a 'key person' who is responsible for the babies' well-being, not just their safety. The key people in this nursery realise that they are performing a parenting role while they are with their key children, playing, talking, feeding, or even changing a nappy. This practitioner holds Baby 3 close to her as she feeds her, maintaining that essential eye-to-eye contact during the feed. She also spends time talking to her two key children, sings, walks them around, and shows them baby toys and other interesting things. Having two little babies to look after is like having twins, but she does a great job, and has plenty to tell their parents when they fetch them at the end of the session.

I'm sure you don't need a prize for guessing which baby will thrive and which will not. Inappropriate, mass care for very young babies, sometimes provided in modern nurseries, with warmth, cleanliness and regular feeding, all in sterile conditions where rows of cots stretch to the horizon, completely misses the most important thing that babies crave: a single person who cares about them. One danger of the recent economic conditions is that mothers who need to work may be forced to leave their babies in this sort of clinical care.

Caring for the individual baby

What babies need is the uninterrupted time of their primary caregivers, and it's not an accident that the distance between a mother's face and her baby's eyes when breastfeeding is the optimum distance for the baby to be able to see her expression and get to know her. This is not going to work if the mum is on her phone, has her eyes glued to the TV, or has propped the baby up with cushions while she does other things.

Attachment happens when caregivers – parents or practitioners – give time and attention to babies as individuals. Even if they can't talk, they can communicate, and it's the job of the adult to try to interpret expressions, gestures, eye pointing and all the other ways babies have of showing their feelings.

Stories, songs, rhymes and jingles are the food of early language development, and it doesn't matter which language is used. Speaking and singing in a higher voice may feel a bit silly to start with, but it really does make babies listen more carefully. Books and stories are also important, it doesn't matter if they can't understand the story yet, the intonation in your voice, and some colourful pictures will help them to begin a lifelong love of books. Babies and children don't need expensive toys. Familiar household objects have just as much fascination for babies, and treasure basket collections, carefully chosen, can offer everything they need.

One of the things we have forgotten in our race to provide everything for our babies is that they do need some time to be themselves. This time should be as secure, yet as free as we can make it, as babies find out about the world around them.

Suitable clothing

Babies are not just miniature adults, and dressing them like adults went out of fashion decades ago. However, it is in danger of returning, as all too often we again see small children in clothing and shoes that ape adult fashion, restricting movement and stopping them feeling, touching, holding and even mouthing everything they can. Tiny trainers and leather boots (and even baby high heeled shoes!) prevent babies from experiencing the world through the hundreds of nerves and muscles in the soles of their feet. As they begin to stand and walk, these muscles will develop more quickly if babies can spend some time in bare feet, sensing the surfaces of hard and soft flooring, steps, slopes and textured surfaces, indoors and outside. This does not mean ignoring safety, but making sure that skin contact is offered as babies learn about the world. Dressing babies in miniature versions of adult clothing also negates the unique nature of the baby and toddler years.

Mari's first months

In our case study, Mari spends time out of doors every day. Even though there is no garden at the flats, Eugenia takes her to the local parks in all weathers, to explore nature and the passing seasons. There is plenty of evidence that babies and young children who experience the world beyond their homes, spend time in the open air, and have space to exercise their whole bodies, will do better when they get to nursery or school. They will be more confident, more interested, and keen to explore and find out about people, places and objects.

Children thrive on contact with other humans, and adults other than their birth parents can provide this, but they need to understand that parenting is not just about changing nappies and filling bottles. The foundations of healthy childhood must be built on the relationships with caring adults who are attuned to babies' needs, spend time in close contact with them, but still allow the growing mind to explore the world and all it contains.

Babies and young children are making more connections between cells in their brains than they will ever do again. Parents and other key people have a unique chance to spark babies' brains into action, getting the building blocks of future learning in place. These building blocks include the foundations of secure relationships, the beginnings of communication and language, and a healthy body fuelled by good diet and plenty of exercise. They will provide the stimulus to building the basic architecture of the brain and body.

The environment for learning

If Mari attends a nursery at this stage of her development, the environment for learning should clearly reflect the needs of very young children. The documentation written to support practitioners across the UK emphasises the importance of each of the factors that are thought to make a real difference between acceptable daycare and exceptional daycare.

Until recently, it was thought that babies could only make secure attachments with their mothers, but we now know that a baby can bond with more than one significant person, and these might include siblings, grandparents, and staff in early years settings, particularly their key person. Secure attachments enable young children to develop positive relationships, and feel secure as they reach out to the world around them, developing a love of learning. Adults in care settings for the youngest children need to base all their work on building relationships and helping children to feel secure. They need to be:

- kind and loving
- consistent
- responsive to children's needs
- capable of building effective and respectful relationships.

The National Guidance for childcare in Scotland advises that practitioners should provide 'calm and safe, but challenging and stimulating environments which offer flexible, individualised and consistent routines'. Practitioners also need to get to know the parents and families of the children in their care, promoting a smooth transfer from home to setting and vice versa. These will include inviting Eugenia to stay with Mari during sessions, and encouraging Mari to bring favourite toys and comfort objects to the crèche with her.

The crèche is staffed by some of the practitioners from the local day nursery. Their crèche room is in the same building, and this will ease Mari's transfer to longer periods of daycare when Eugenia feels she needs it.

Child-sized provision

The best settings for babies and toddlers have elements of familiarity, as well as new experiences and resources. The crèche that Mari will attend has been furnished with home-like objects – a settee, a couple of armchairs, carpet and curtains. But there are also some things that Mari will love as she becomes mobile – child-sized chairs and tables, a toddler-sized home area with plates, cups and saucers, little prams and trucks to trundle around, dolls and soft toys, and above all, more small children to play with. This gentle introduction to other toddlers will be very beneficial to her language development as well as to her learning. Very young children don't seem to notice what language their friends are speaking, they appear to take more notice of actions, expressions and body language, so it will be a good place for Mari to expand her understanding and speaking of English.

Time for stories, songs and nursery rhymes, a small snack time, space out of doors, and a place for a nap if they need it, will also meet the needs of this group of children. These activities are the basis for stimulating language, relationships, and a sense of fun and enjoyment, which are the best stimuli for lifelong learning.

Although attachment and attunement are at the heart of high quality provision for babies and toddlers, this is not enough on its own. Practitioners know how a stimulating environment can trigger future learning, and the adults in care settings for babies and toddlers observe the children regularly, responding to the emerging needs of individual children, and using their observations to plan activities that meet the interests of individuals and groups. Spending time with babies, and watching their responses are keys to providing a rich and stimulating environment within which the brain can grow. It has recently been found that an enriched environment can have a visible physical effect on brain development within 48 hours, so Mari is lucky to have high quality provision in her local area.

A world of wonder awaits Mari. She feels confident and secure, and she is alert to the possibilities of every experience she faces. She is handled with gentle love and kindness, and rarely becomes stressed or unhappy. What a great start to life!

A message from Mari

I can move around and may seem to be very independent, but I still need my mum or another familiar person to be nearby at all times. I love meeting new people and playing with new toys, but please make sure I have time to get to know new people before you leave me. I will often choose to play with things from my mum's handbag or the kitchen cupboards, and really like my new treasure basket, which has lots of exciting objects to play with, pick up and explore. I respond with smiles and waving to music, songs and nursery rhymes, especially if they involve movements such as clapping and pointing. I am learning new words all the time, and I can understand far more than I can say.

Practitioners

- Make contact with parents before their children start at your setting or school, not just to collect information, but to make a firm foundation for the key person relationship with the child and their family. How can settings for babies find time for this?

- Children who learn two languages in their early years often do well at school, particularly in reading. Families are moving around the countries of the European Union much more freely than ever before. How can you make starting nursery or school a successful experience for the children of these families?

- This is the stage when children are learning words at a faster rate than they ever will again. The number of words babies understand always far exceeds the number they can say. Lots of songs, rhymes, and time to talk will all help. How do you make time for your own key children?

Parents

- Sing songs and nursery rhymes in any language to help your child with reading and talking.

- You don't have to spend lots of money on expensive 'baby toys', objects from your home, offered to your baby in a treasure basket will stimulate their learning and concentration more than highly promoted 'learning toys'.

- By this stage, your baby will be very attached to you, and may respond to other adults by crying or clinging to you. This is normal, don't let your anxiety show, just be gentle and understanding, and the behaviour will pass.

- Mother and baby groups, such as Mari's Baby Club will help both you and your baby to meet other people and make relationships. This type of contact will also help your child to learn to talk, and the second and third years are key times for learning to communicate with other children and adults.

Interlude 2 Three chemicals and chimp management: chemical influences on the brain

'As science gains greater insight into the consequences of stress on the brain, the picture that emerges is not a pretty one. A chronic over-reaction to stress overloads the brain with powerful hormones that are intended only for short-term duty in emergency situations. Their cumulative effect damages and kills brain cells.'

Franklin Institute

As we move on, and with the experiences of Max and Mari in mind, it will be helpful to look at the chemicals present in human bodies. These are produced in every human body and brain, but their balance will be affected by the unique mixture of nature, nurture, culture and chance given by the throw of dice at conception and in the years that follow. More than 100,000 chemical reactions go on in the human brain every second, and we need to be sure that the chemicals in young children's brains give them the best chance of responding positively to the world about them.

In the womb, Max's body was bathed in amniotic fluid, and through this fluid ran the placenta, his link with the outside world through his mother. Since her birth, Mari's body has consistently contained a higher level of calming chemicals, serotonin and oxytocin, a balance that results from the environment in which she lives. Because of this chemical balance, she will be more contented, responsive and confident as she explores her world.

There are thousands of different chemicals whizzing round our bodies all the time, but let's concentrate on three of them, which I think make a difference to how children learn. Managing the balance of these three, and the way they act on our bodies provides a vital tool in the educational toolbox. These three are myelin, cortisol and serotonin.

Myelin: practice makes perfect

Myelin is a chemical substance, which forms an insulating layer round the connections between neurons (brain cells) protecting and strengthening them. Myelin is white, and its colour has resulted in the scientific description of the difference between the 'white matter' in the brain – the myelin coated links between cells, and the 'grey matter' – the cells themselves. In human brains, the white matter tends to be concentrated in the centre of the brain, with the grey matter close to the skull.

The importance of myelin has already been discussed in earlier chapters. It is a fatty, chemical substance produced by the body when an action or reaction is repeated, and the links between brain cells are re-visited, particularly as a brain practises something new. It is laid down every time a route between cells is repeated, and it helps to protect the 'soft wiring' of initial experience or skill, insulating it in the same way as the coating on a cable insulates an electrical signal. Myelin winds round the vulnerable links until they are converted by practice into 'hard wiring' the skills, knowledge and understanding that we have embedded in our brains. Walking, driving, making a cup of tea, riding a bike, and swimming are all myelinated activities, we have done them so many times that we don't even have to think about how to do them. Practice has in fact made perfect!

Developing associations

Imagine trying to remember the name of a new colleague, a tall, slim, newly qualified teacher we'll call Rachel. Your brain needs to form an association between a complex visual image and a name, each of which is encoded by different groups of neurons in various parts of your brain. When you first meet her, you lay down links between what you see (her face), what you hear (her name) and the fact that she looks a bit like your next-door neighbour. Every time you meet Rachel now, these sets of neurons fire simultaneously, strengthening the synaptic pathway that connects them. Soon, when you spot a tall, slim woman coming down the corridor, you will easily greet Rachel because the visual image will be strongly linked with the sound of her name. What is happening in your brain is myelination, and the more often you meet Rachel, the firmer your knowledge of who she is will become.

If you watch a small child for any length of time, you will be able to actually see them myelinating the links in their brains. They persist in climbing up a ladder and down, up a ladder and down, putting objects into a post box and tipping them out again; they fill and empty buckets and bags, wrap objects and unwrap them, drop objects from their high chairs and watch them fall, over and over again. These are all explorations into the world, early scientific experiments, and they are often referred to as schemas. Schema behaviour is evident in most children until they are about six, although it does continue for longer in some people, and even adults retain some schema activity, such as transporting things in handbags or throwing their children into the air for fun, or obsessively ordering the cans in a food cupboard or their collection of DVDs.

Some of the schemas you may see as you watch young children are:

- Transporting – carrying toys and other things around, in containers, pockets or just their arms.

- Enveloping – wrapping up dolls or teddies, or draping themselves in cloaks or sheets.

- Enclosure/containing – posting things in post boxes, filling and emptying boxes and cups with sand or water, sitting inside boxes, washing baskets or cupboards.

- Trajectory – diagonal/vertical/horizontal – dropping things from their cot, kicking a football, throwing toys, jumping off the furniture.

- Rotation – a fascination with things that turn, the washing machine, doorknobs, wheels, swings and roundabouts.

- Connection – joining things together, such as a train track or Lego, exploring masking tape or string.

- Positioning – lining cars up, putting sticks in rows, or even wanting their food in very separate places on the plate.
- Transforming – changing things, making potions, mixing spills on their plate, adding water to the sand.

If we look carefully at children's behaviours, we can see myelination in action everywhere as children repeat activities again, and again and again, fixing the process or exploring the action over and over again until it is hard wired in their brains.

Myelination is more likely to occur when babies and children are free to choose their own activities and concentrate on them for periods of time. Babies and children seem to know which links they need to work on, and if we provide a range of open-ended materials, they can choose the ones they need. That is why a treasure basket is ideal for sitting babies who can choose and explore the objects that appeal to them at the moment – putting a stone into a small metal tin and tipping it out again, waving and twisting a small metal whisk in the air, spinning the wheels on a little wooden car, wrapping a fir cone in a small piece of fabric, or stroking their own hand or leg with a small brush. Every time a child says 'Again!' they are probably exploring a new schema.

Self-initiated play

As babies get older and are able to move about, schema play may be less obvious, but it is still there in most children. We see toddlers and under fives wrapping themselves in fabrics, rolling balls down slopes and tubes, riding round and round on a tricycle, going endlessly up the ladder and down the slide, and of course the endless connection and disconnection of Lego, the train track or the roadway. All these activities are myelination in action!

Schema play for older children, throughout their primary years, can also involve many of these open-ended resources, although, once children are on the move, they may use them in very different ways. 'Loose parts' for exploratory play for older children will include: drainpipes and guttering, boxes and crates, planks, baskets, buckets, leaves and cones, sticks, stones, sawn logs and shells in quantities that enable children to build, construct, recreate and imagine as they learn to work and play together.

The popularity and value of such play has been recognised in schemes such as Scrapstore's Play Pods, an initiative which provides playground collections of recycled, loose parts resources, like those described above, for use at lunchtime in primary schools. Free play with large quantities of these materials has resulted in much more positive behaviour, fewer accidents, and has had an impact in the classroom where teachers are reporting that children are coming in from lunchtime ready to learn, and much more interested in creativity, science and technology. Of course, what a Play Pod gives older children is an opportunity to play and practise at their own level with resources that have many uses. In this way, babies and children can become young scientists, exploring and experimenting with found and natural materials, with adults available when they need them. In the past, such activities might have been referred to as 'junk modelling' or 'free play in construction' and were an essential part of the day and the week for children until the age of seven. In the current climate of ever increasing pressure for adults to provide evidence of progress for each child, this sort of play may be squeezed out by more formal, teacher-directed activities, leaving children with partial or insecure learning processes. Practitioners and their managers need to think about the purposes of these activities and the vital nature of their contribution to brain development.

Long periods of time for self-initiated play are essential for myelination, allowing children to repeat activities that help to fix learning links in our brains, and children who have plenty of free play with open-ended materials make complex patterns of wiring in their brains. Myelination is a fascinating process, one of the few learning processes that we can see in action, and support by providing appropriate toys and other resources. Without the magic of myelin, everything we did would seem to be done for the first time, and even if we had done that thing many times before, no trace of it would remain in our brains.

Learning would be an easier process if we could rely on a course of simple soft-wiring, turned into hard-wiring through repetition, and in fact that is how it happens in the best of all worlds. Babies like Mari and Max have a better chance than many others to build their learning in this way, but other children's learning processes are open to a dangerous attack by other chemicals in the body.

Cortisol: chemical attack!

There are three major stress chemicals in our bodies: adrenaline, norepinephrine and cortisol. These chemicals are all produced in our bodies in response to stress. The first two are instant response chemicals, switching on the response of 'flight, fight or fright' when something stressful happens, and we need to respond quickly, for example, a child runs into the road, someone bumps into your car, you think you are being followed at night. In these situations your body can provide you with extra energy, speed and strength to snatch the child from the road, jump out of your car, or escape from the stranger.

Cortisol takes a bit longer, minutes rather than seconds to have an effect on our behaviour, because the perceived threat or stress is checked out across the brain before the body starts to manufacture the chemical. All three chemicals affect learning, because as they respond to the perceived stress, they damage and destroy the myelin protection on the learning links in our brains.

Babies in the womb start to produce cortisol and other stress hormones before birth, but if the pregnancy is normal and relatively stress free, the balance of these is automatically kept at a manageable state, and the baby will not produce these hormones in significant quantities until after they are born. However, babies who experience the effects of too much drinking, drugs or smoking by their mothers, or who sense her stressful life, will respond in the womb and will be born with higher levels of all sorts of damaging stress hormones, many of them harmful to brain development.

The problem with stress chemicals is that they are sometimes difficult to control and during our lives some children and adults can get 'stuck' in a circular process of manufacturing these chemicals, specially cortisol, in response to stress. In these individuals, stress affects the brain, cortisol is produced, and this, in turn, raises the level of stress, which results in the production of more cortisol. Some children, particularly those with stressful home lives, or those who are not doing well at school, can get into this circular process and produce enough cortisol to prevent them from learning anything.

Cortisol is produced in and released from the adrenal gland, and flows quickly through the body and the brain. It gives an almost instant 'fizzing' response to stress, particularly when we are threatened, giving us the option of 'fright, fight or freeze', discussed earlier in this book.

The chimp in us all

Steve Peters is a sports scientist who coaches professional athletes and sports people. In his book *The Chimp Paradox* (Vermilion), he describes the function of the human brain as a sort of dance between three characters:

- There is a computer which collects and stores all our myelinated learning, helping us to keep track of all our experiences, and organising these in a way that allows us to retrieve them quickly and easily. The computer remembers our name and the way home, keeps track of the people we meet, and spends time between waking and sleeping to tidy up and put away new information or reorganise the information and learning we already have.

- The second character is a chimp that is the remnant of our ape ancestors, with a chimp's natural responses to the stresses in our lives, this character responds to the stresses in our lives and can sometimes over-ride the computer.

- These two characters might end up in a constant battle for dominance, but a third character has power over them both. This is a human, with human instincts and emotions. The human manages the conflicts between the computer and the chimp, keeping order, sometimes more and sometimes less effectively.

Computers are orderly, organised and predictable, chimps are notoriously unpredictable, noisy, spontaneous and irreverent, and each person's chimp is different from every other chimp in the world. This makes chimp management difficult, however endearing the chimp may be, and is complicated by the sensitive job of managing chemical levels in the body and brain.

Steve Peters, who works with elite athletes, suggests that the way we learn to manage our individual chimps, each of which has a different ignition point when put under stress, is what makes us uniquely human. While reading his book, I began to think about the chimps we see in young children, and the job that parents, practitioners and teachers have in helping children to manage their own individual chimps. Firstly, we need to know what it feels like when our chimps take control.

Take a look at these situations and think about how your individual chimp might respond. Would your chimp over ride you, and become angry, aggressive, violent, jealous or rude? Or would your chimp be amenable to calming reason from the human in your brain, and show understanding, humour or sympathy?

How would you react?

- You are in a traffic queue, and a van overtakes you, cutting in on the queue. How does your chimp feel?

- You are in the line at a buffet, your favourite sweet is éclairs, and someone jumps the queue to grab the last remaining éclair.

- You are in a staff meeting. One of your colleagues is giving very detailed feedback about the course he has recently attended. Just as he finishes the feedback, the deputy head says, 'Now, we need some ideas and volunteers for after school activities?' Your friend catches your eye and makes a funny face.

- You are driving along a local road and you see a parent hit their small child across the head.

- You are at a football match and the opposing team fouls one of your players. The referee doesn't see the foul and allows the player to go on and score the winning goal.

- Your partner has promised to be home in time for you to go for a drink with your best friend who you haven't seen for ages. Your partner is late and their phone is switched off.

Of course, some of these situations will enrage your chimp more than others, but would it be different if you knew that the van driver was taking his wife to the hospital, or the child had just run into the road and nearly got run over, or your partner had been discussing a possible redundancy with their boss?

Childish chimps

As adults we are experienced in managing our emotions, and calming our chimps so they don't get out of control too often, specially at work. Young children don't have the benefit of adult experience, and they often let the chimp take over. When they are under stress, they leave the thinking part of their cerebral cortex behind and descend through the cerebellum into their old reptilian brain, resulting in those primitive, extreme behaviours of temper, violence, tantrums, confrontation or tears where the child is in 'flight, fight or freeze' response. We all know children who respond acutely to stress, particularly those who experience extreme family violence by retreating into silence and stillness to avoid more exposure, and some children who even appear to smile when under stress, despite the fact that this behaviour is sure to make things worse.

Learning to manage stress comes with maturity and experience, combined with the management of a very specialised part of the brain called the amygdala. The amygdala is an almond shaped cluster of neurons located deep in the centre of the brain, which has a 'gatekeeper' role in managing our emotions, permitting or preventing stress to drive our behaviour down into the old reptilian part of our brains, where the simple responses of 'flight, fight or freeze' lie and the chimp is waiting to respond. Children and adults who have not learned to control their responses will be at the mercy of the amygdala. Their reactions to stress will always be extreme and often without thought – and the chimp wins!

The stress chemicals in our bodies ebb and flow as we manage our chimps each day, hopefully better than many children do. As adults we have learned to control our behaviour, remaining in the thinking part of our brains where logic and understanding lie.

Conflicting effects

Stress chemicals, and especially cortisol affect our chimps, <u>and</u> they actually erode the myelin we have carefully built up on the links in our brains. The more cortisol we make, the more learning we lose. Cortisol is particularly good at eroding recent myelination. Here's an example:

Understanding the conflict between myelin and cortisol might help us to challenge the thought that some children are less able than others. It is quite possible that some of these children are not intrinsically less able, they may just need more repeats before they have hard wired the learning, particularly if stress is continually eroding the production of myelin. If we criticise or otherwise put stress on them by suggesting that they are unable to learn, we will prevent them from ever producing enough myelin or fixing it in place – the chimp wins yet again as these children withdraw, refuse, challenge, misbehave or dissolve into tears!

Good stress/bad stress

I hear you say, 'Isn't it good for us to have a bit of stress? Doesn't stress stimulate us to be assertive, to stick at things, to be alert and inquisitive?' The answer to all of these is – Yes, we do need to experience stress for all sorts of reasons, not just to trigger our flight from crocodiles or shout at football matches.

Scientists have looked carefully at the different sorts of stresses we experience, and they have devised a definition of stress in childhood by describing three different levels, and each of these interferes with learning in different ways:

1. **Positive stress**. This is the sort of stress that makes us resilient and able to stand up for ourselves. It's the sort of stress children have to cope with when they go to the dentist, have an injection or lose a game with friends. The stress may have an effect for a few days, but most children cope with this sort of stress relatively easily, and it gives them practice in managing their 'chimps' in everyday small stresses, building up resilience for more extreme events or the next dental appointment.

2. **Tolerable stress**. This second level of stress is experienced by most children at some time during their childhood. The death of a close relative or a family pet, family breakdown, serious illness or moving to a new school. These events are painful at the time, and may affect learning for short periods, but with support and close comfort from family and friends they can be managed, even though they may leave scars. A child can even endure and recover from the effects of something as terrible as a tsunami or an earthquake if they have support from others and can see a secure future. Children who have had experience of positive stress will manage these 'tolerable stress' events more easily. Their chimps are used to being managed and calmed by reason.

3. **Toxic stress.** This is the highest level of stress experienced by children. Some children live with this sort of stress every day, and it can have a permanent effect on their lives, leaving them unable to function properly as children or later, as adults. Toxic stress results from persistent poverty, neglect, lack of stimulation or abuse, and particularly if these come in combination. Children experiencing these stresses cannot function normally, even if they have a secure environment at nursery or school for part of the day. Their bodies are producing so much stress that they are unable to concentrate or to engage with learning, and importantly they will not be able to remember things, as the stress of their home lives rapidly undoes any learning they have done. In fact, just thinking about what might happen at the end of the day will affect concentration and focus, even in engaging practical activities. Such children can become withdrawn or very demanding of the positive attention they crave so much – their chimps are out of control!

Stress for young children

However hard practitioners and parents try, stress is present every day for very young children who are cared for out of their homes. The natural place for babies is with their mothers, and just the hand-over between mother and carer raises the level of stress in babies (and often in their mums too). Making the nursery setting as welcoming and home-like as possible will help babies to transfer calmly.

If, in nursery and early years settings, there is too much restriction, too much sitting and listening, not enough free choice or outdoor play, and too much adult directed activity, levels of stress will inevitably rise. Children will be attempting to manage the stress, their chimps will be responding in many different ways and the whole situation can be out of control. Stress management is an art, not a science, and every adult gets it wrong sometimes. Managing the balance between no stress, positive stress and tolerable stress is a large part of the job of a parent. early years practitioner or teacher because it is possible to trigger 'reptilian brain behaviour' in any situation. The wonder of it is when we watch an outstanding practitioner or teacher as she or he manages a large number of early childhood chimps.

Helping children to manage the chemical balance in their bodies and brains is the key to learning as well as to stress management. Another is to encourage the manufacture of the third chemical in our trio – serotonin – which can help to reduce the effects of cortisol and the other stress chemicals while supporting the manufacture of myelin.

Serotonin: cool and blue

Serotonin could be called the 'swimming pool' hormone. When we look at the clear blue water of a hotel pool in a holiday brochure, the majority of us will begin to manufacture serotonin, the feel-good chemical. We begin to feel happier as we remember our holidays; our memories affect our bodies and our muscles relax. Calming chemicals flood our brains. One of these is serotonin, which reduces stress and encourages feelings of well-being.

Serotonin also has a role in managing sleep, appetite, memory and learning, and has a part in preventing depression. It works in our brains, supporting the transmission of information between brain cells. In fact it is a substance that has more diverse actions in the body than any other.

Making serotonin

Serotonin is not naturally present in our bodies, so we have to manufacture it from the food we eat. This is done in our digestive tract and in the pineal gland located in our brains at the top of the spine. Serotonin is made from foods containing tryptophan, an amino acid, so we should all eat a diet containing plenty of foods high in tryptophan, to keep our serotonin levels high, and a diet rich in fruit, vegetables, proteins and essential fats will provide this.

We can also manufacture serotonin from sunlight, and understandably, specially in northern countries, our serotonin levels can vary during the year, with lower levels in the winter, sometimes contributing to depression or Seasonal Affective Disorder a condition which improves as light levels increase in the spring, and the pineal gland can manufacture more serotonin from the increased daylight. This is another reason for children and adults to be out of doors as much as possible.

Helping children cope

Young children need our help to produce serotonin, as it really does counteract the effects of stress chemicals such as cortisol. Of course, when a child has an active 'chimp' or when they are so distressed that they can't think of anything else, we need to wait until they have retained their composure before starting on the process of making serotonin. One way to do this is by using the natural responses to a stressed child, which are the ones that help them to begin the process of making their own serotonin. Holding, stroking, gentle talk and even singing are natural responses, but the same strategy will not be effective for all children or for all circumstances. Holding and calming, removing the child from the centre of attention, counting to ten, deep breathing, and reasoning are all effective methods of helping children to restore the chemical balance in their bodies, and children should learn as soon as possible which techniques work for them.

When children are hungry, thirsty or tired they often have those irritating and irritable chimps near the surface, and resolving these problems with something sweet to eat or drink can speed up the process, and give the child time to recover their equilibrium. Strangely enough, one of the most effective foods for calming chimps and supporting serotonin production is a banana!

After a difficult or frustrating experience, we all need time to take control again, and while they are young, children may need considerable adult support while they do this.

Healthy food choices

Because food has such an effect on feelings, part of this support will obviously involve looking at children's diets, both at home and in any setting they attend. This will help them to keep their levels of serotonin buoyant, with a resulting effect on their ability to 'manage their own chimps'. A diet high in essential fats, vitamins and minerals from plenty of fresh fruits and vegetables will support serotonin production, as will whole grains, fish and white meats, such as turkey and chicken.

On the other hand sugary drinks, refined sugars, white flour and processed foods, inhibit the production of serotonin, and as adults, we should also reduce the amount of caffeine and sugar substitutes we drink (most readers will be pleased to hear however, that dark chocolate has tryptophan). A lack of exercise depletes serotonin, so plenty of fresh air, activity and sunlight will also help in 'chimp management', and some early years settings have supplemented the low light levels in winter by changing to daylight bulbs.

To summarise this interlude, parents and practitioners should be aware of the effect of chemicals on brain growth and behaviour, both of which affect learning.

- Myelin protects the learning.
- Cortisol erodes myelin.
- Serotonin can help to achieve balance between these two effects.

Children need help to manage the stresses in their lives, and their personal 'chimps', and we need to develop management strategies for them, even though they may not yet understand what is happening to them. A healthy diet and exercise, with plenty of daylight and fresh air will help, not just to combat obesity, but to achieve the optimum chemical balance to help them succeed.

Points to ponder

- How could practitioners and teachers ensure that children have enough time during the day to practise and consolidate their learning through play?
- Some stress is inevitable, and some may even be positive in helping children to become resilient. How could settings and schools manage their work so children achieve a good balance of cortisol and serotonin during sessions, and at times of transition from home to setting?

- How could practitioners help children who are experiencing more dangerous levels of stress in their lives, such as the break-up of parent relationships or permanent poverty? These children's stress levels are likely to be overwhelming for much of their day. How can we help all children to be aware of and manage their chimps?

- We now know that the level of 'feel good' chemicals such as serotonin in our bodies depends on the foods we eat. Children who are hungry, thirsty or tired can't control their behaviour and responses to others. How can managers of schools and settings offer information to parents and adults, and the staff of school meals and out of school provision, so they can provide the right foods for the children and for themselves?

Stage 3 A brain on legs – Sam is just three years old

'Like sleep disturbances, some worries at separation can be expected in the second year. If you accept this, then you will avoid reacting to this anxiety as if it's your fault. A mother who feels guilty will appear anxious to the child, as if to affirm the child's anxiety. By contrast, a parent who understands that separation anxiety is normal is more likely to react in a way that soothes and reassures the child.'

Cathy Templeman, journalist

Between 12 months and three years, children change dramatically. Reflect on Mari in the last chapter – unable to move herself about and get the things she wants, unable to communicate in words, unable to choose the things she wants (and doesn't want) to eat – apart from slamming her mouth shut. In the next two years, she will develop into a walking, talking, exploring individual, able to control her own body and use her growing language to develop her thinking skills.

Sam's story

Sam is just three. He has attended nursery for some time, and has recently started a full-time place, which is proving to be a long and tiring day for him. He lives near the school, with his parents who both work full time, and his two sisters, Bel and Beth, seven-year-old twins. It is October.

Sam is standing by the nursery door, waiting for someone to come and fetch him. He is a small, stocky child, with blonde hair and big brown eyes, which at the moment are beginning to fill with tears as he sees the last nursery children leaving with their parents. Cortisol is kicking in, his breathing is getting faster, his heart rate is increasing, and he will need help to keep his responses in control. The 'flight, fright, freeze' mechanism is triggered as Sam feels abandoned.

However, help is at hand. Sam's key person, Jan, comes over and sits him on her knee, gently stroking his back with her hand. She knows that Sam's mum is often a few minutes late, as she has to collect the twins from the school next door, and the teachers there aren't as flexible as the nursery practitioners.

'Mummy coming?' Sam asks Jan, 'Home now?'

'Soon,' says Jan, 'She's just collecting the girls. I know you are feeling sad, but she will be here soon.' Jan is used to Sam's questions, he always gets anxious about transitions from home to nursery and nursery to home, a common feature in boys of his age. A good sign is that Sam feels this separation anxiety at both ends of the day, so he obviously feels as secure with Jan as he does with his parents, it's just the transitions between the two.

Jan asks Sam if he wants to choose a book to read while they wait for Mum, and he goes to the book corner, returning with his book of the moment – *The Gruffalo*. Books with rhymes and a sense of rhythm really engage two and three year olds, and he joins in as Jan begins to read the story to him.

'Jussaminit,' he says and he runs off to fetch the Gruffalo finger puppet from a basket in the book corner.

'Readit now,' he says. He puts the puppet on his finger and waggles it as Jan reads.

Sam's language development is not causing any concern in the nursery, but there is a slight delay, as there often is when a child has older siblings, who often speak for them, and in the case of Sam, double the trouble with a pair of very articulate sisters! Sam is also a 'summer born' child, with a birthday in August. He will always be the youngest in his year group, almost a year younger than his friend Ben, born the September before him.

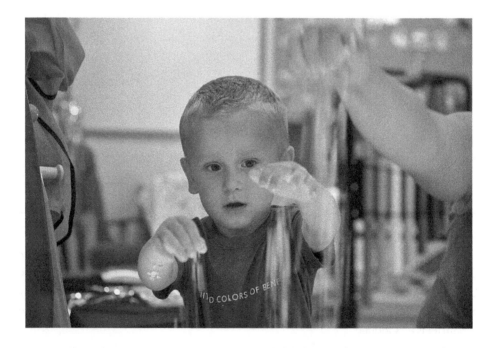

Sam loves books and stories. His sisters have always shared books with him, and are just getting to the stage when they can read the text in familiar picture books, so the bedtime stories are going to help Sam's language development even more. He has a loving relationship with his sisters, who have mothered him ever since his birth, often treating him like a doll, but also lifting some of the load of parenting from their mum and dad. Chris, their dad, is a self-employed bricklayer, and he has to find his own work, which is not always easy. The result is that Di, their mum, has taken on more hours at the superstore, sometimes working extra shifts in the evenings and at night. This doesn't help Sam's confidence, as he sometimes doesn't know who will fetch him from school.

The Gruffalo story is finished. No one has come. Jan suggests that Sam might like to get the train track out. She knows this is a favourite, continuing Sam's interest in connecting and disconnecting. Using schema play often helps a child to feel more secure, the repeated actions and familiar toy help to distract him. Jan goes over to the phone and contacts the head of the school. He is sitting in his office and the twins are there too. No one has fetched them either.

Jan suggests that the twins should come to the nursery room to play with Sam while they all wait, and soon they burst in, very pleased to come back to a place they remember with fondness. They quickly go into the home corner, where they start to cook and sort the equipment. They try to fetch Sam from his train set to be the baby, but he doesn't want to. He is now old enough to say 'No' to his sisters, and he plays in the home corner during the day when he can be the boss! As they play, all three children begin to sing. They love singing and their mum taught the girls lots of nursery rhymes, which they have now taught to Sam. The girls move round the home corner, singing, and lightly clapping their hands in time to the song. Their singing moves seamlessly from song to song, as the twins go through their family repertoire.

There seems to be a bond between twins that enables them to communicate without talking, although no one knows for sure whether this is nature, nurture or culture. The chance of being identical twins means that the girls share many characteristics, including a very similar genetic pattern. However, the latest work on the human genome has found that even twins have subtle differences in their genomes that may make their lives significantly different from each other, even if their upbringing appears to be identical. Even though they look so similar that only their mum can tell them apart, they may suffer from different inherited diseases or conditions, and their lives may turn out to be quite different. Studies on twins separated at birth and brought up in different families in different cities, have discovered that some traits (subtle things, such as wearing their watch on their right wrist, or always wearing blue button-down shirts) may appear in both twins even though they have not met since birth.

However, even in twins brought up together, traits such as sociability, job preference, allergies, or marital status appear to be more randomly affected by genetic changes, nurture, culture or a different set of life chances.

Let's go back to Sam. He has suddenly realised that it's getting dark outside. He's only been coming to nursery in the afternoons for a couple of weeks, and he doesn't realise that the autumn evenings are drawing in. He can see the street lights at the end of the path and he begins to weep again.

Then suddenly he yells, 'Daddy!' He sees his dad, rushing up the path, and into the nursery, out of breath and apologising to them all. Sam bursts into floods of tears of relief. The twins are less excited, they would have been happy playing here for much longer. This shows how their strong relationship with each other, as well as their attachment to their parents give them confidence that someone will come, and meanwhile, Jan will look after them.

Chris had completely forgotten that it was his turn to fetch the children. He had been at the pub at lunchtime and a friend had told him about some work in the next town. Chris had hopped on a bus, and by the time he had found the right building site, talked to the foreman, and got back, he had totally forgotten about the children. It was only when he walked into the house, ready to tell everyone his good news that he noticed the quiet, looked at the messages on his phone, and remembered. He walks over to Sam, but Sam shouts at him 'I don't like you Daddy!' and starts to punch Chris's legs before sliding to the floor in a weeping heap. Both Chris and Jan know the tantrum is caused by the sudden release of stress, which Sam was not able to cope with. Chris picks him up and sits down to comfort him before apologising to Jan and taking the children home, knowing he will get a real talking-to from Di when she gets back.

How is Sam getting on?

Sam is still a two-year old at heart and this is making it difficult for him to settle to full-time nursery. He is used to having the afternoons at home with his mum or dad, sometimes having a short nap or watching TV, then going to the park for a football game, or playing in the garden, where he enjoys being on his own and not being bossed around by his sisters. He gets very tired at nursery all day, and is worn out by home time. No wonder he 'lost it' when Dad was late.

The sense of independence that comes with being two was late arriving with Sam, and he still enjoyed the afternoons of doing his own thing in the garden or indoors, making dens, climbing, swinging, and digging in the flower beds, where he can sometimes be persuaded to help his mum with the weeding, although he is much more likely to pull up the things he shouldn't. His love of the outdoors shapes a lot of his learning, and he still spends much of his time at nursery in the garden.

Dealing with separation

Sam is experiencing separation anxiety when he is left at nursery, and taking some time to settle, even with Jan, who has been his key person since he started nursery at 18 months. Boys are more likely to experience this anxiety than girls, and it needs to be handled sympathetically, not by telling them to 'grow up' or 'be a big boy'. This is one area where culture is still evident, and however much we believe in equality between the sexes, there are still expectations that boys will not show their feelings as much as girls, and don't need to be comforted. The evidence says that boys feel just as strongly as girls, and sometimes more strongly, particularly about their mothers. As a society, we expect boys to be stronger and braver than girls, and to need much less touching, hugging and physical reward. Research shows that even when they are tiny babies, we tend to touch boys less, hold them for shorter lengths of time, and look into their faces or smile less often than we do with girls. Perhaps we feel that boys need somehow to be toughened up and masculinised, but in fact this behaviour seems to make boys more fragile, not less. Boys who are lovingly held, cuddled, stroked and smiled at become more emotionally resilient, and better able to cope with stress.

Although Sam's parents are loving and kind, they are busy, and have left some of the child-rearing to a pair of inexperienced yet well meaning sisters, who alternately treat him like a doll, or play the 'good mum/bad mum' alternately shouting and criticising him, even when he is doing nothing wrong, or smothering him with hugs and kisses. This leaves Sam even more confused.

Slow developers

However, Sam is a fairly typical just-three-year-old boy. His physical development is within the normal range and there are no major concerns about him. Jan knows he was a premature baby and this sometimes affects physical development and learning in the early years. In fact if Sam had been full term, his birthday would have been in September, and instead of being a 'summer born' with all the disadvantages of being the youngest in his year group, he would have been among the oldest children in the next year group, yet another of life's chances, and a warning to schools that they should not jump to conclusions about maturity or ability without all the information. Clever schools log information such as month of birth and premature babies, and refer to this information alongside current feedback from observations and assessments.

One of the difficulties faced by premature babies is that they have had less time in the womb to get ready for birth, so they may be later to accept solid food, later to crawl, stand and walk. When children start school, 'late blooming' can be a double issue when a child is also born during the summer months. They have less time in the womb, and less time out of the womb to practise learning, so the links in their brains have thinner coatings of myelin, and are more susceptible to erosion.

Many children can fall into the category of slow developers and there are almost as many reasons for this as there are children. Here are some:

- Some 'late blooming' is a genetic trait, inherited from a late blooming family. If you suspect this, talk to the family about their own childhood, and you may find some late blooming parents.

- Physical or emotional problems or illnesses in the early months can result in a pause or delay in development. Make sure you have all the information about the child's developmental and medical history, and that you use this information when making judgements about individuals.

- Either for 'heritable' reasons, or following early illness, some children, may be smaller, and smaller children are often, although not always, developmentally delayed. These children can also suffer from being 'babied' by parents, siblings and other children at nursery or school. Look carefully and sensitively at such children, understanding individual circumstances does not mean lowering your expectations.

- For all sorts of reasons, which may include lone parenting or only children, delayed social development can result in a child seeking younger friends, who are like them in needing more time to grow up.

- Some children have later blooming muscular development when compared to their peers. This can affect their large or fine motor skills, hand-eye coordination, hopping, cutting, catching a ball. Of course, this does not include the perfectly normal behaviour of under fours, called 'overflow movement', where a child sticks out their tongue when drawing, or flaps their arms when climbing stairs. Late muscular development, which may include later control of bowel and bladder functions, is worrying, but it is surprising how many of these children catch up later, particularly if the problem is not 'over emphasised'.

- Some children (and Sam is one of these) have delayed language development. This will get in the way of learning, children with delayed speech at two are at risk of problems later when faced with reading and writing.

- Children who often get noticed immediately, have a much shorter attention span than expected, and find it difficult to sit still and listen. This attention delay or deficit is a problem for children and adults, and although all young children may suffer this at times, professional help may be needed. Later in this book, in Interlude 8, I talk in more detail about attention.

- An interesting delay in some children, and one that is not always recognised, is later development of the ability to stop doing something they are interested in, and find it very difficult to conform to some of the expectations of nursery life. Experienced practitioners recognise this difficulty and use gentle techniques to encourage the child to put a toy away or join a different activity, using music, songs, or a timed warning to indicate an imminent change of activity.

Language development

Like many boys, Sam's language development is behind that of many girls of his age. This is normal, as language processing goes on in both sides of the brain, and girls generally have more links through the corpus callosum between the right half and the left half of their brains, enabling them to process speech more easily. Most girls, by three, have moved ahead in speaking, listening and understanding language, and by the age of about four and a half, girls have enough left/right brain links to begin the complex process of learning to read. Boys develop later, and some boys with perfectly normal brains are seven, eight, or even older before they have equivalent brain structures for the highly regarded skills of reading. Boys and girls are not better or worse than each other, they are different, developing in different ways at different rates.

Male brains appear to major on right brain structures in their earliest years, they are much more interested in active learning with their whole bodies. Many girls develop the ability to sit still, focus and concentrate at an earlier age than most boys and this means they can start on the complex task of learning to read at an earlier age.

Like all his family, Sam loves music. His dad plays guitar in a local band, and Sam is very proud of him. The children always go to his 'gigs', even though his mum is sometimes working. The girls look after Sam, jigging about with him and encouraging a sense of rhythm and beat, which will give him a real advantage when he starts to read. Children with good 'beat competency' learn to read more easily, and children without it may struggle for years to become fluent readers.

Exploratory play

At nursery, Sam continues his interest in outdoor play, climbing, riding bikes and playing with his friends, mostly Ben, who is older and more confident. Indoors, he will choose to play with bricks, construction toys or the train set, sometimes joining the home corner play. Sam's key person, Jan, understands that his play at home is dominated by the twins, so she is keen to give him freedom to express himself, make his own friends, and take control of his own play. She is not worried about his slightly delayed speech, as he listens intently to stories, retells them as he plays with small world figures, and can handle books with care and confidence. He loves books with rhymes, rhythm, and repeated phrases, and joins in when she reads these.

She also 'eavesdrops' on his conversations with other children, and particularly when he uses puppets, as in these activities he seems more confident to speak at length. Some less confident children communicate more easily when they are speaking through a puppet, doll, soft toy or other character, and Jan often uses this technique at group times to encourage Sam to contribute.

Because Sam is more interested in active play, Jan will be planning some large motor activities that involve mark making and fine motor control. She has several children in her group who need this practice, so she will gather them together for short periods to make patterns in dry sand with their fingers, use play dough to strengthen their hand and finger muscles, follow her movements using ribbon sticks or rhythm blocks, or use tools in soap suds or shaving foam. The children love these activities and they are all available for free choice, but Jan watches carefully to find out which children don't choose these activities, and she targets these children in a group session where she can model the play and encourage them to develop the skills they will need for writing. Sam's pencil grip is still a 'fist grip' so, now he is developing a dominant right hand, she will gently encourage him to use a tripod grip (with two fingers and thumb), which will make writing easier and faster for him as he grows up. Habits learned at this age will stick, and bad habits can get in the way of efficient learning.

Switching on learning for two and three year olds

Play, preferably with plenty of space, interesting resources, and adults as play partners is the ideal recipe for two and three year olds. Children at this age are still pushing the boundaries, finding out what they can do, and spending time pursuing their own interests. If adults are not careful the unpredictable signs of the 'terrible twos' and even the 'terrible threes' can erupt, to everyone's dismay. Tantrums and outbursts, behaviours born of frustration, continue in boys beyond the age when girls appear to lose the need and this is certainly linked to language development, something where most girls have forged ahead at this age leaving many boys behind, unable to say what they mean, want or feel. Development of the slower-growing left hemisphere is faster in girls, giving them the edge in language and in managing their behaviour and that of others through reason, persuasion and even guile!

Testing the boundaries

Many children's tantrums result from the frustration of not being able to express themselves, and what they want, to others in words. Combine this frustration with the urge to be independent, to do things for themselves, and to test the boundaries of behaviour and relationships, and a remaining feeling of being at the centre of the universe, the only important person, the only one with rights, and you will see the problem. Cortisol builds up and explodes in violent behaviour, shoving, hitting, grabbing and other behaviours that are unacceptable in a childcare setting. And of course, when a child is in the middle of a tantrum, they are in no position to listen to reason, they need a chance to calm down, in a quiet place away from attention or with a trusted adult. Until they have regained their equilibrium and are calm enough to talk through what has happened, an audience is the last thing this behaviour needs. Many settings are now involved in programmes for helping young children to manage their relationships with others – the Conflict Resolution training by High/Scope is one example. These programmes help children to talk through their problems with adult help, instead of resorting to physical responses.

Empathy, the ability to understand and respond to how others feel is not a genetic ability, even though some families seem to be able to teach it to their children more efficiently than others. Empathy needs to be learned, and does not really become embedded until children are at least seven. Sam and his friends are still taking their first steps on the way to managing their own emotions, so Jan spends a lot of her time helping them to do this by talking through conflicts and differences, knowing that time spent now will be worthwhile later, as children develop interpersonal and social skills. Of course, Sam's immaturity means that he may take longer to learn these first steps in empathy, although his twin sisters are good role models for him.

Coping with cortisol

The last Interlude, looked at stress chemicals and the effect they have on the brain. Frustration is one of the feelings that trigger the manufacture of cortisol, and some of the frustrations of two and three years olds are:

- Not having the words to say what they want.
- Not being mature enough to understand sharing or ownership – the concepts of 'mine', 'yours', and 'ours' may be slow to emerge.
- Lacking the ability to wait for a turn, a ride, a toy.
- Not understanding other people's point of view, and that the other child feels just the same ownership.
- Being tired, hungry or thirsty.

Learning to be in a community and to work with other children is very tiring, and Sam is feeling the strain as he moves to a full-time place at nursery and his freedom is restricted further. Jan makes sure that all the children have free access to drinks, water at all times, and sometimes milk or diluted juices. There are frequent opportunities for children to have a small snack, at a rolling, self-service table with fruit, vegetables, crackers and toast. Key practitioners have a responsibility to check that their key children are taking advantage of this 'little and often' snacking, which seems to suit young children's bodies. Sam is one of those who doesn't seem to know when he is hungry or thirsty and needs a reminder to eat and drink. He will probably get used to the rolling snack within a few weeks of full-time nursery, and this will remove one of the reasons for stressed behaviour.

Types of play

Jan and the other practitioners in Sam's nursery know that they are very powerful supports to children's learning, and that the complex role of teacher, observer and co-learner is a very sensitive one, as they scaffold children's learning and respond to what they see the children do. Sometimes a practitioner will be a *play partner*, joining in the play as an equal. This could involve them in being the baby in the home corner, helping to build with the bricks or race with cars, kicking a ball in a football game, or being the audience for a story told by a child.

Sometimes the practitioners will be *parallel players*, playing alongside, mirroring the child's activity, modelling and talking about what they are doing. At other times, they will be *observers*, collecting information about children that will help them to plan more activities or enhance learning by following children's interests, perhaps by adding new stimuli, additional resources, stories or creative ideas. This could be as simple as providing red, blue and black paints for boys interested in painting superheroes, borrowing more building blocks from another group to extend the fantastic village built by a group, or helping the children to collect leaves, sticks, stones and pebbles from the garden to make a Gruffalo small world area in a builders' tray.

Sometimes Jan and her colleagues will initiate *sustained shared thinking*. This is a process where an adult joins a group, listens and watches to see what is happening, and then gently joins the play, usually by contributing to the conversations between children. This is one of the most difficult but rewarding elements of the practitioner's 'toolbox'. During these sessions, Jan is very careful not to dominate the conversation, but she will offer comments, questions and suggestions that will help the children to think more deeply about what they are doing. This is not adult-directed activity or teaching, Jan does not want to change the direction of the children's play, she has no 'learning objective' except to encourage the children to think about what they are doing, and what they are learning.

As children get more used to adult participation in their learning, they are able to cope with more adult-led activities, where the practitioner uses familiar and specific resources for more structured activities with clear objectives and a purposeful direction to the session.

As Sam moves up the school, he will continue to experience this subtle interaction with adults, sometimes in child-initiated activities, sometimes in small group time, and later in short sessions focusing on thinking skills, and eventually activities where the adult has control, while still working within the same environment. The whole school, which takes children from two to 12, is committed to a thinking skills approach, where children are not just learning, they are thinking about learning, and, better still, thinking about thinking (otherwise called *metacognition*). In later chapters, we meet older children engaged in thinking about thinking, a powerful tool for both young and older learners.

Between two and three, children are learning words faster than they will ever do again, but as we have seen, sometimes these words are blocked by emotions, and the need to do things straight away. Adults need to understand this behaviour, staying watchful, continuing to be a safe haven when things go wrong, but enabling children to become independent in their activities and their learning.

The environment for learning

Easy access to resources is a key to supporting independence, and when he fetched the puppet, Sam showed that he knew where to find things. Frustration is reduced when a child can find what they need without having to know the words, and anyway, it is now evident that sometimes children don't know what they want to play with until they actually see it – visibility is the key to switching on myelination. At Sam's age, smaller quantities of equipment, with several baskets of the same thing, will reduce friction among groups with dominant personalities and a limited commitment to sharing.

Because children of Sam's age are still making vast numbers of links between brain cells, and revisiting these again and again, offering resources that switch on schema behaviour – things that connect, turn, fly, move, make marks, fall and envelop are still as important as they were to Mari as she explored her treasure basket. 'Loose parts', those everyday resources with no single purpose, are still important, but Sam and his friends have moved beyond the treasure basket, except for an occasional themed collection brought together by adults to explore a theme or topic such as Colour, Wheels, or Fruit, when a basket of items helps children to explore the topic in free play. Loose parts for Sam are indoors or in the garden, planks, guttering, tubes, ropes, tyres and crates out of doors, and collections of reels, buttons, plastic tops, tins, pegs, and other simple items are available for continuing *heuristic play*.

Children need places where they can practise what they see adults and other children do. Home corners and other role-play areas continue to be very important in exploring the world, and other simple role-play resources such as superhero capes, fire and police props, hard hats and wheeled toys are combined in familiar and unusual ways. Comfortable places to read books and make marks all contribute to a sense of continuity where exploration and experiment can take familiar resources into new learning. This is why the successful settings for two and three year olds are very similar to successful settings for younger children.

Learning next steps

During this stage, good practitioners observe the children they work with, and watch what and how each child is learning, which skills they are acquiring, how they are relating to others. They will also be looking at 'next steps', the next things children might need, new skills they may need to develop or learn. This process, called *scaffolding*, involves adults in watching children as they play, and helping them through the door or up the step to the next stage of learning. Sometimes the adult will decide that the children need more than a play partner playing alongside as an equal, some new resources, or an inspiring story to take their learning further, they will need a teacher. This does not mean that the children sit and the teacher teaches. It means that the adult takes the lead, being a model, shaping the play by deciding the purpose of the activity and matching it to the needs of individual children. These activities will probably look very much like those chosen by children independently, what is different is the way a skilful practitioner uses familiar resources such as sand, water, bricks, puppets, paint and other staples of the early years to guide the brains and bodies of individuals and small groups of children, so they can confidently take the next step in learning.

Supporting new skills

If we waited for children to learn how to use scissors, pencils, hammers or other tools on their own, it would probably take a long time, and there would be many mistakes and false starts on the way. To be successful, children need help and support, particularly as they learn new skills, watching the adult demonstrate new and more familiar tools, trying simple processes first, then having a go themselves, before using the tools in self-chosen activities. It may be that feeling the hand of the adult over their own as they gently guide the child's fingers, can be the best way to success. This process is not only useful for teaching tool-use, it is the way adults teach children other things. Talking, counting, singing, using a computer, playing a game with rules, reading a story, everything is better if children have a good model to follow, as well as being able to try things on their own.

When planning activities, getting the balance right between activities that will be led by adults and those chosen by children is a sensitive and professional task. Too much adult intervention will result in frustration for the children; too little may risk missing critical windows in children's development. Too little child-chosen activity can result in poorly myelinated links in the brain, which may fall away from under-use, leaving children over-dependent on adults; too much child choice can result in what has been described as 'hands on, brains off' activity where children are not really learning much.

As children go on through the education system, the balance of child-chosen and adult-planned tasks changes, with more time spent in adult direction, and less in self-chosen activities, which, by the time children reach adolescence, have been reduced to the status of homework or hobbies, both taking place out of school.

If Sam and his friends do not spend enough time making and myelinating links in their brains before the age of eight or nine, some essential skills and abilities that are not firmly in place may never be so, leaving children as poor readers, un-coordinated writers, and particularly, inexperienced thinkers for life. These children are in no position to make the best of their education, and they will be unlikely to have fulfilling jobs. This waste of potential is nothing short of a crime, and an over-emphasis in government policy, education guidance, and inspection, and on direct teaching, instead of supported learning, will only make the situation worse.

'Trying to speed learning over unfinished neuron systems might be akin to racing a car over a narrow path in the woods. You can do it, but neither the car or the path ends up in very good shape!'

Jane Healy

The right curriculum

The written curriculum guidance, the Early Years Foundation Stage (EYFS) for the support of young learners, across the UK and particularly in England, reflects the best of research and knowledge about child development. However, the current political will is often at variance with what these documents advise. Science tells us that children thrive on a practical, engaging curriculum which responds to their individual needs and interests, but constant pressure from government to achieve ever higher standards in a narrow range of competencies only serves to reduce the curriculum to a 'one size fits all' garment that is actually suitable for only a few. Schools and settings are constantly bombarded with misinterpretation, personal opinion and politically biased instructions, which often contradict the findings of the scientific community worldwide. Rote learning, direct teaching, unreasonable expectations, regular testing, prescriptive inspections and damning public reporting are undermining the will of good practitioners and teachers, as they try to balance what they know is right with the demands of politicians, who often have little experience of the real job of teaching and learning.

In many countries across Europe and the world, children do not start formal education until they are six or seven years of age. Before this, they experience appropriate, play-based, first-hand nursery provision, often with much time spent out of doors, where they can explore and learn at a pace appropriate to the developing brain. In such countries, by the time children enter school and a more formal learning programme, they have had time to build a strong architecture of myelinated links, a basis for future learning in a more structured environment.

Most children in the developed countries of the world have an opportunity to attend some kind of pre-school provision. In some countries this is arranged, provided and paid for entirely by parents, and there is no outside intervention in what is provided. In these countries provision is very varied.

In most countries, however, the government has some role in defining good practice in pre-school provision and in monitoring the schools and settings. Within the countries of the UK guidance is provided by each government, as is the curriculum for children of statutory school age. In England, there are now detailed descriptions of the Characteristics of Effective Learning (CEL) for children from birth to around five years of age (when children enter school). This guidance emphasises the need for play and practical experience, balanced by appropriate adult intervention, suggesting the provision should ensure that children become and remain:

- *engaged*, through playing and exploring
- *motivated*, through active learning
- *thinkers*, by creating and thinking critically

. . . and that these engaged, motivated thinkers should be supported by *Positive Relationships* and *Enabling Environments*.

In Sam's nursery, and in the Reception class that he will move into next year, the practitioners have taken this guidance seriously. They have discussed the CEL in detail, and even though they felt that the match with their practice was good, there were things they should incorporate into their daily practice to achieve an even closer match. Here are some of the indicators Jan and her team chose to examine, and what they decided to do in response (CEL statements are in italics):

- *Provide stimulating resources, which are accessible and open-ended so they can be used, moved and combined in a variety of ways.* A good look at what was happening in the nursery resulted in a decision to take cupboard doors off, bring resources out of cupboards, and make a photo book of the resources that they didn't have space to display all the time, so the children really do have choice.

- *Ensure children have uninterrupted time to play and explore.* This meant looking at and changing some of the fixed points in the day, such as snack and outdoor times as well as planned group times, to ensure that children really could have long periods of uninterrupted play.

- *Keep significant activities out instead of routinely tidying them away.* Even though the staff knew that they had more space than many settings, and could keep more activities out all the time, there was still long discussion about what 'significant' meant, and which resources really were 'significant' to the current group of children.

- *Children will become more deeply involved when you provide something that is new and unusual for them to explore, especially when it is linked to their interests.* The practitioners found that they had to observe the children even more closely to find out their current interests. These are now logged in the planning folder so adults can refer to them in their planning, and activities such as role-play and small world play can change to reflect emerging interests. They also collect and offer 'objects of interest' such as an interesting piece of wood, a glass vase, a Christmas tree bauble, a small character figure, a piece of jewellery, a huge key, or a new story book, to stimulate discussion or pick up on a current interest of individual children or groups.

- *Build in opportunities for children to play with materials before using them in planned tasks.* Before new or unfamiliar resources are used in a planned activity, they are talked about and demonstrated to the children. Then the new resources join the general resources in the setting for free access before using them in group activities. In this way, children are familiar with them, and are not distracted in adult-led activities by the excitement of new resources.

- *Play is a key opportunity for children to think creatively and flexibly, solve problems and link ideas. Establish the enabling conditions for rich play: space, time, flexible resources, choice, control, warm and supportive relationships.* This statement is checked regularly against what really goes on in the setting, and any problems are discussed, so children have enabling conditions for learning.

- *Recognisable and predictable routines help children to predict and make connections in their experiences.* The practitioners make time for children to adapt to new situations, and try to keep the nursery routines as consistent as possible.

This final statement brings us right back to Sam. He needs the security of predictable routines so he can move on from his current anxiety, and really engage in learning.

A message from Sam

I was looking forward to being three, and spending all day at nursery, but sometimes I get very tired and wish I could have a nap on the settee. Don't leave me there too long, come to fetch me when all the other kids go home or I will get very angry with you, even though I still love you. You are still the most important people in my life. I love Bel and Beth, but sometimes I wish they wouldn't treat me like a baby – I'm a big boy now!

For practitioners

- Boys are more vulnerable than girls, but often our culture expects even very young boys to be stronger, braver, and more able to cope with separation than girls. What could you do to change this cultural behaviour, and to recognise the tension between growing up and still feeling vulnerable?

- Boys develop more slowly in emotional, language and cognitive development. Do you provide for this in your settings and schools?

- At this stage of development, many children still need regular snacks. How do you manage this in your setting or school?

- How are we managing to support children whose fine motor skills or language development are causing concern? Do you explore the possibilities of a genetic link, where late blooming may be a family feature, which just needs patience and understanding?

- Children at this stage are immersed in repetitive schema play, domestic role-play, and 'loose parts play', and may become very stressed when they have to stop for the routines of the educational day. How do you track and build on children's current play interests by providing resources, activities and time to support their current interests?

For parents

- Remember that from birth, we tend to touch, cuddle and praise boys less than girls. Boys need our approval and love just as much as girls do, even if they seem more able to manage without us. Do you treat your sons the same way as you treat your daughters?

- Children all need consistency and reliability, and it was a good job that Jan was able to stay with the children until Chris arrived. Make sure your children feel secure and that you remember how important you still are to your children. Separation anxiety can have a long-lasting effect, and boys feel it more than girls.

Interlude 3 Everything by mouth: talking and eating, the issues

'Talking is a hydrant in the yard and writing is the faucet upstairs in the house. Opening the first takes the pressure off the second.'

Robert Frost, poet

'If we taught babies to talk as most skills are taught in school, they would memorise lists of sounds in a predetermined order and practice them alone in a closet.'

Linda Darling-Hammond, Professor of Education, Stanford University

Sam's key worker has noticed that his language is a still delayed. Not enough for intervention by a speech and language therapist, but enough for Jan to watch and record any problems he has in communicating with other children and with adults. She knows that children who have severe language delays in early childhood may catch up with specialist help, but may also have problems later with reading. However, as an experienced practitioner, Jan needs to collect some more information before she acts.

When Sam was in part-time nursery, Jan had already noticed the delay, and she now intends to do the first stage of support for him – in-school support – which will start with some focused observations to find out exactly what the problem is. Jan has already talked to Sam's parents, who, being very used to two chattering girls, feel that Sam must be very delayed, and were very apprehensive when Jan asked to talk to them, but also relieved that their growing concern was not just an over-reaction. Jan explained that many boys are later than girls in developing language, due to different rates in the growth of boys' brains, both in the womb and during early childhood. She asked whether Chris or Di had been slow to talk in childhood. Di knew that she had been an early talker, her mum had commented on the twins' non-stop chatter and told Di they were just like her at that age. Chris can't remember, but he said he would ask his mum. He can remember being a late reader, and was conscious of this when he was about ten and had to read out loud to his class.

Jan knows that there can be a hereditary factor in learning language, and suspects that she knows what Chris' mum will say about Chris and his early speech. This information will help the professionals to make a diagnosis, and they may come to the conclusion that Sam's language delay is a hereditary condition, which will improve over time. Meanwhile, Jan will recommend that the twins try not to baby Sam, or speak for him, and the whole family will encourage him to sing, clap, talk and take a bigger part in conversations at home. Di, Chris and the twins all need to give him more time to respond, something that may be difficult for the twins!

If Sam's language problems persist, specialists from speech therapy, speech and language support and nurture groups may be involved. The majority of children involved in such therapies are boys, and this is almost certainly due to the late development of the left hemisphere of the brain in male children. Boys are often later to talk, to read and to get involved in writing, and this can lead to more pressure on them to achieve unrealistic targets when they are simply not ready. We need to recognise that boys learn by doing, and need to be physically active to learn effectively, and even to talk. If you watch children carefully, they are constantly on the move, even when we think they are sitting still. Some of this movement is due to immature muscle development, but in some children, particularly some boys, it is a necessary part of any activity, including speaking and listening.

Language skills from birth

At birth, girls have made more links between brain cells within the left hemisphere, where language is processed. They also make more early links through the central corpus callosum between the two hemispheres, enabling language areas in the right and left hemispheres to communicate with each other, sparking language responses all over the brain. At one time, scientists thought that language was entirely processed in a few small areas in the left hemisphere, particularly Wernecke's area, where words are understood, and Broca's area, where they get ready to be pronounced. These two areas are not very near each other, and the connections between them take time to develop, so it's no wonder that babies and young children can often understand what we are saying long before they can say the same words themselves. We also know from more recent research that language is processed all over the brain, and is managed in different ways by boys and girls, and by individuals within each gender.

Scientists are now certain that the beginnings of language development occur in the womb. These beginnings include an essential sense of rhythm, or 'beat competency', which later develops into the ability to recognise and hold a steady beat. Try it yourself and see how well you can keep a steady clapping rhythm, adding a song or poem once you have established the beat. This ability is first experienced in the womb as the baby hears her mother's heartbeat and the pulsing of their shared blood through her ears.

This ability to recognise and hold a steady beat is essential to all language development. Even before birth, and before babies can understand the meaning of the words they hear, they listen carefully to the rhythm of the language they hear. Different languages have different rhythms, so Mari will need to adjust her listening skills from the rhythms of Spanish (her first language) to the subtly different rhythms of English. In nursery and early years groups, many practitioners now nurture the ability to hold a steady beat by including rhythm activities in their daily routine. They may offer the children simple blocks, rhythm sticks or even chopsticks so they can add a beat to nursery rhymes and songs, adding to this activity by marching, stamping, turning and bending as they keep the beat. Many songs and finger rhymes include clapping or other movements, but practitioners don't need to stick to these, they clap along to any song they sing. This is what twins Bel and Beth were doing in the home corner, as they continued to clap along to the simple tunes they are singing. This has become such a habit that, for the rest of their lives, they will probably continue to clap, tap, rock or nod to any music they hear.

Babies whose mothers (and fathers) sing to them in the womb also seem to be more attuned to language, and will often turn to look at the source of the same voice or tune when sung after birth. Some television theme tunes or adverts appear to be just as catchy to babies as they are to adults, and very young babies may respond to music or songs that they heard when their mothers swayed, sung, or just relaxed as they listened to radio or TV.

Once babies are born they start to look intently at faces, and even very young babies will follow a simple drawing or puppet of a human face as it passes in front of them, preferring this to any other pattern. This natural fixation with human faces has triggered some new research into language development, which indicates that babies learn to talk by lip reading, carefully watching the faces they see, then copying the movements. Psychologists now say 'Don't worry about what babies hear you say, worry more about what they see you do!'

What babies can immediately see and will then learn, are the shapes of our lips and faces, particularly when we say consonants. Specialised brain cells respond to these movements and the baby, unconsciously at first, attempts to copy them, sometimes without a sound.

Try making these sounds silently – 'm', 'b', 'd', 'n', 'g'. These are some of the first purposeful sounds that babies make as they babble those repetitive consonants, and we recognise them with such joy as their first words – linked, usually accidental sounds that we interpret as mamama or dadada. Our pleasure in these first recognisable sounds will trigger the baby to repeat them. Serotonin floods parent and child, and the baby laughingly repeats the sound again and again, strengthening the neural links in their brain and their facial muscles, so that next time, the baby may be able to make the sound more purposefully. Late at night or early in the morning, if you listen to a baby when they are alone, they will often be practising these sounds to themselves, a workout for the brain and the muscles for talking, with the added boost of a shot of serotonin when they see you smiling.

We tend to speak more slowly and clearly when we are talking to babies, and this may be an instinct that helps babies to see what we are doing. It is also instinctive to hold a baby near our face when we speak to them, and a distance of between 16 and 20 cm appears to be the optimum for babies to see and begin to imitate our speech.

Mirror neurons

Another recent finding that appears to help babies to copy adults as they speak, is that the human brain contains some very special cells that appear in the brains of humans, and to a lesser extent in higher apes, dolphins and some dogs, but not other animals. These cells are called mirror neurons, and some scientists think that they enable us to make links in our brains without having to actually perform the movement or activity we see. For example, when we see a dancer on TV, our mirror neurons will respond to the dancer's movements, making similar neuron links to those going on in the brain of the dancer. We don't move, but our brain 'mirrors' the dancer, reinforcing those neural paths, which as we watch the dancers more and more, making structures in our brains that enable us to even predict what the dancer's next steps will be. It would be great if we could become professional dancers or footballers as we sit watching them from the settee, but unfortunately our mirror neurons don't extend their influence that far.

Mirror neurons do respond to movements and expressions that other humans make, enabling us to 'feel' and remember the movements they make. It also seems possible that mirror neurons affect our ability to empathise with others' feelings, expressions and even their words seeing and understanding what others are feeling. Most women, who from girlhood, have watched the faces of the people near them, will have had much more experience of empathising. Boys, who are less interested in people and watch them less, will often have a lower response to the feelings of others, and some find it puzzling that girls can do it so well. 'Watch my face,' is a request that we hear often in early years provision as practitioners give boys direct practice in using those mirror neurons.

Children with Autism are now thought by some developmental psychologists to have imperfect or 'broken' mirror neurons, and this may help us to understand the condition better. Work in this field includes the application of knowledge from the HGP, where scientists are investigating the influences of heredity on a whole range of conditions, including Autism. Perhaps, sometime in the future, we will find a way to switch off the gene that triggers Autism.

Developmental pathways

The slight but important differences in the development of children's eyes, their ears and their brains all affect the development of language, and boys have a different developmental pathway from girls. These differences will affect their ability to learn for the whole of their lives, starting with the expectations of daycare and the early years in school. Boys' brains are not different in overall structure, but different parts of their brains develop at different rates, and by the time they enter the education system, most boys excel in gross motor skills of climbing, running, swinging, jumping, riding and rolling. The finer skills of writing, reading, speaking when it's their turn, and listening to others (and particularly to the teacher) will be less developed than the girls in the class. Boys have spent less time talking, more time moving, less time listening, more time doing, less time watching others and more time thinking about the next adventure. Whole-group activities are really difficult for many boys at this age, and their delay in language development often becomes obvious at this time. Many boys by three are still not speaking in sentences, but can follow quite complex instructions and speak confidently in two or three word phrases. Sam's problems are with speech production, and Jan wonders if he was too reliant on a pacifier when he was younger. She will ask Di when she next sees her.

As explored earlier, girls are more sensitive to voices, particularly their mother's, and they respond better to face-to-face conversation (getting more experience of lip-reading); they talk earlier and tend to master the skills of reading and writing at an earlier age, often finding phonics and 'sounding out' of words easier than most boys. Girls generally have better hearing, can concentrate for longer, and have fewer language disorders such as stammering or delayed language. One of the keys to early talk is an interest in watching other human communication, and girls tend to be much more interested in people and what they are doing. This means they have a desire and motivation to talk, and because they spend more time near or with adults, they get more response and modelling from them.

Seeing

All children need to have binocular vision so they can move with confidence, coordinating the muscles in their eyes so the two images are exactly fused into one. The child who needs to rest on other children's heads as they negotiate their way across a group seated on the carpet, or shows other signs of physical clumsiness, probably has not perfected binocular vision. Difficulty with interpreting facial expressions is another sign of immature vision, so if you give a child 'the look' from the other side of the room and they don't respond, it may not be that they are ignoring you, they may just be too far away to interpret your subtle message of gentle correction. Good vision will also help them later to differentiate between letter shapes for reading and writing. Due to the later development of coordination of the left half of the brain, some children may take time to manage this, and may squint to get a more stable view using just one of their eyes.

And hearing

Children also need to develop 'stereo hearing', the ability to hear equally well with both ears, so they can tell the differences between sounds and in the nuances of speech. Again, this may develop earlier in some children than others, and those who seem to lack concentration may just be finding it difficult to hear you. Encouraging these children to sit near you may help.

Perhaps because sound differentiation is difficult, and develops more slowly in most boys, they will tend to use whole-word recognition as their major reading strategy, only mastering phonics later, as their hearing becomes more acute. As part of her preparation for assessment, Jan will ask Di to arrange for Sam to have a hearing test to establish whether he has temporary hearing loss, or 'glue ear'.

Windows for language

In general, children's language develops from cooing and crying, grunts, cries and squeals in the first four months, and babbling during the next four months, to the use of words, first as single utterances at around 12 months. This is the point at which the tentative sound of 'mamama' can be interpreted by a mother as a call to them in person.

Between 12 months and three, there is an absolute explosion in the learning and use of new words, mostly nouns and verbs, which are refined and combined in twos, threes and longer phrases. These follow the rhythm of the child's first language, and often consist of linked sounds that mimic words, sentences, songs, phone calls etc. By the time a child is four, they should have a vocabulary of between 4,000 and 6,000 words, a wide knowledge of the rules of putting these together, and most of the rules of conversational speech, although the conventions of taking turns in conversations sometimes fail. Children from more affluent families will naturally reach this stage, but it is now evident that many children who live in poverty will be at a disadvantage, with a more limited vocabulary and lower levels of communication skills such as listening and complex speech.

Practitioners and teachers know that there are particularly sensitive periods in the development of children's brains, when there are windows for learning particular things. The learning of a first or a second language is easier in the early years, and particularly before four years of age. As babies learn those first 'babbling' sounds, there is no difference in the sounds a French baby, an Indian baby, or a Chinese baby make, they all make the same range of sounds. However, as the baby hears language, and starts putting these sounds into words, they gradually prune the sounds that are not part of their first language, and it becomes difficult to recapture these later. It is therefore useful to remember that children who live in England, or who need to speak English in school should embark on learning this as soon as possible.

Bilingual learners

Many of the children in Sam's nursery have English as their second language, and many are bilingual, so their vocabularies may contain all 4,000 words in their first language, or a mixture of two or more languages. The practitioners are very keen to celebrate and recognise each child's first or mother tongue, so they include songs, rhymes and stories in the many different languages represented in their community. However, they know that the children will need to learn English, as their education and future working lives will demand fluency in this language, even though they may continue to speak another language at home. This means that during most of the day, practitioners are modelling English, with dual languages and community languages used in group times and stories. The children speak a mixture of languages as they play together, and appear to be able to understand each other most of the time. When there are disagreements, the practitioners will lead the discussions in English, translating the children's responses if necessary, so everyone understands.

Children who are bilingual, or who learn a second language when they are young, may be slightly delayed to start with, but they soon catch up. Jan and her colleagues have been trained in language development, and they try to maintain a balance of valuing all languages and making sure all children have opportunities to learn English at an appropriate level.

The key to language

So what are the keys to learning language and communication? Firstly we need to understand the difference:

- language is about the words, the vocabulary, the grammar and syntax of using a language;
- communication is as much about behaviour as just the words, and children need to watch and listen, watch and listen again, to learn how to communicate.

To be successfuly communicators they need to learn the language of the body and face as well as the voice, and some children who have spent long periods watching screens and not people, may find they need more practice to become capable communicators. A child's ability to develop language depends on being immersed in a rich environment of words, sounds, rhythm, and verbal and non-verbal expression from their earliest years. They also need a wide range of opportunities to use these skills, and Jan's nursery is a rich learning and language environment, where children have time to talk, listen and learn in different groups at different times. They are surrounded by print, in books, labels, posters and notices, they hear stories and rhymes in a range of languages, and explore rhythm and rhyme using simple instruments such as rhythm sticks, wooden blocks, bells and shakers. Their phonological skills are honed through listening and sound games.

Confident practitioners know that learning to communicate is built on a need to tell our own stories to other people, and hear their stories too. They give young children lots of opportunities to tell the stories of their lives and activities, both at home and during a busy day, and they encourage parents to share the stories of their own lives with their children. Learning to communicate, to have a conversation, to listen to other people, to show empathy and interest are all essential skills for life.

Becoming readers

Learning to read is an even more complex task and should not be rushed. Reading can only 'float on a sea of talk'. Immersion in print and stories will not be enough, children's brains need to be ready, and getting them ready needs lots of 'hands-on' play to ensure that eyes, ears and brains are prepared, and lots of talk to ensure that what they read is meaningful. A child will only be able to write a story when they have:

- Understood that stories are everywhere, in real life as well as books, and they can tell them too.
- Made up their own stories and told them to their friends.
- Listened to stories and retold these, in role-play or with puppets and small world figures.
- Played the story of family life in the home corner, drawn the story of their visit to the cinema in a picture, felt the story of Spiderman and the villains on the climbing frame, rode the story of the pizza delivery on a bike, swum the story of Nemo as their hand swished in the water tray, talked the story of their birthday party, or grandly paraded the story of the princess in a shiny bridesmaid's dress.

Young children don't just learn by listening, they need to experience things with their whole bodies, and in lots of different ways with lots of different resources, and effective early years settings hum with children telling stories. Many of these are about real people and real events, interpreted in different ways by different children, just as we retell the stories of our lives to friends and families, interpreting them from our own unique standpoint.

Stories told by adults, with or without a book, real or imagined, will make a valuable contribution to reading, as will high quality picture books, but spoken language is at the heart of all learning. Without language we can't think, plan, solve problems or communicate effectively. Learning to communicate with others takes time and practice in the company of people who are interested in what you have to say, and in Sam's nursery, as in all nurseries, there is a consistent focus on language development, on speaking, listening, and on understanding.

The pattern of early language

The pattern of the child's home language (their mother tongue) is learned as they hear their mother's voice through the tissues of her body, and other voices from outside the womb, including those they hear on TV and on the radio. Raised voices and arguments heard in the womb will trigger the production of stress chemicals in the baby as well as their mother, and the impact of these raised voices will remain after birth, in raised levels of cortisol in the baby. Babies subjected to violent voices in the womb are often smaller and more anxious than babies who hear mostly calm and loving speech. It is evident that one of the keys to successful language development is to maintain a calm and supportive environment, and Angie, Eugenia and Di all tried to provide this for their unborn and newborn babies. Later in this book you will meet other children who were not as lucky, not just experiencing *language delay*, but *language deprivation*, where a child learns to communicate in spite of living in a linguistic desert, where they may learn more from the TV than from real people.

Food for thought (a side dish)

I have said before that the brain, the most important organ in our bodies, works by chemical reaction. Manufacturing myelin, serotonin, oestrogen, progesterone, and many other chemicals, to say nothing of those stress chemicals! It is like having a great unconscious chemistry set, with our brain at the centre, managing things for us. What is really amazing is how often it works in our interests and how relatively rarely it goes wrong, continuing to keep us alive in spite of our worst intentions.

We all recognise the contribution that a diet rich in fresh foods and whole grains makes to learning. Well-fed children make more progress, stay on task for longer, have more stamina and are less likely to be disruptive or cortisol-laden. However, some children's lives are not so rosy.

According to a survey of 5,000 UK adults commissioned by Save the Children in 2013:

- Nearly two thirds of parents in poverty (61%) say they have cut back on food and over a quarter (26%) say they have skipped meals in the past year.
- One in five parents in poverty says they cannot afford to replace their children's worn-out shoes, while 80% of parents in poverty say they have had to borrow money to pay for food and clothes over the past 12 months.

The Joseph Rowntree Trust (in 2013) says food shortages are now on a scale not seen since wartime rationing. Food prices have spiked across the world but in Britain, where we import around 40% of our food, prices have risen at more than twice the EU average and families are struggling to afford food that has increased by 32% since 2007.

In some settings and schools, many of the youngest children now come to nursery or primary classes without the advantage of a good breakfast, and their parents can't afford the cost of Breakfast Club. The School Fruit and Vegetable Scheme may provide a small nutritious veggie snack (but no carbohydrates for stamina) halfway through the morning. With a packed lunch at dinner-time, often of dubious nutritional value, at the end of the day, these children return home for a ready meal or takeaway if they are lucky, bread and jam or a packet of crisps if they are not. One headteacher recently reported a nine year old arriving in the dinner hall with a whole Swiss roll in her lunch box – nothing else, just a Swiss roll – which she said her mum had got as a bargain from the local supermarket.

How can these children ever compete in the learning stakes with the most fortunate of their classmates, with their warm coats and shoes, whole milk and whole grain breakfasts, balanced and nutritious packed lunches, and evening meals with their families in well-heated houses?

What does this tale of poverty and disadvantage have to do with language development, and what does it have to do with learning? The answer is 'everything'. And, sadly, even more affluent families have lost the habit of buying fresh, cooking at home and eating with their children. We are all in danger of being dominated by fussy eaters, limited palates, and children who won't eat anything green!

Fussy eaters

I was sitting at a table in a holiday hotel a year ago, sipping freshly squeezed orange juice and watching the other holidaymakers coming from the breakfast buffet, plates loaded with all sorts of goodies they normally wouldn't allow themselves. One young man attracted my attention. He sat at a table hunched in deep concentration, systematically removing all the pulp from his orange juice with a fork, and discarding these 'bits' in a saucer. The process took some time, before he was satisfied that the juice was clear, and suitable for his taste. I wondered whether this young man had spent a whole childhood avoiding the bits in food! Children like him insist on a diet that can be sucked and swallowed, soft enough to be squashed between their tongues and the roofs of their mouths, sucked from straws, plastic pouches, or already mashed. Add to this diet of smoothies, bread from refined white flour, that dissolves in the mouth rather than needing chewing, over-cooked or tinned pasta, beans or ready meals of soft pies, mashed potato or rice.

Compare my holidaymaker's eating habits with Mari at her meal, eating the same things her mother eats, using her fingers to pick up small pieces of fruit and vegetables, practising her pincer grip, chewing the bits of fruit in yogurt, or the 'al dente' spaghetti in its sauce, enjoying the colours, flavours and textures of the finger food she is offered.

Weaning and talk

But what has this to do with language development? I hear you ask again. Well we now know that children who continue to eat smooth food throughout their toddler years talk later and less clearly. The first mouth movements that babies practise are sucking, but sucking only exercises cheek, tongue and throat muscles. Talking needs us to manage our teeth, tongues, lips, cheeks, jaws and face muscles together, and chewing gives us much of the practice we need for talking. That is one reason why children with severe speech and language difficulties may be given a feeding programme as part of their treatment plan.

Many children, like my 'bit fisher', are now coming into nursery and school having never eaten food with lumps in it. We are told that the child will refuse any food with lumps, and will only eat food the consistency of mashed potato or custard. These habits can continue into late childhood and even adulthood, as we have seen. 'No bits' babies turn into 'No bits' teenagers, and into 'No bits' adults, as a baby fad becomes a lifetime habit, influencing the shopping and eating habits of whole families.

It seems probable that one of the ways that parents switch on this aversion to lumps is by starting weaning too early (before the 'around six months' guidance) and this is too early for the baby's immature digestive system, risking infections, allergies and an aversion. There is also some evidence that too early weaning can result in childhood obesity and heart problems later in life. Parents must remember that you shouldn't start weaning a baby until they can stay in a sitting position and hold their head steady; coordinate their hands, eyes and mouth (i.e. can grab food and put it in their own mouth by themselves); and swallow food that is not liquid. Babies who push the food out of their mouths again may not yet have the mouth muscles to push the food to the back of their mouths.

The best way to encourage a wide palate is of course to start young, and introduce a variety of flavours and textures. Babies and young children are influenced by what their mother ate while they were in the womb, by the foods they see their family eating, and by little tastes of these foods as they reach that 'six months' threshold. The wide range of baby and toddler foods available can bedazzle parents who are themselves influenced by what they ate as babies – if they ate bananas and baby rice they may never think of buying peach, avocado or butternut squash.

What can we do?

As practitioners or teachers, we may feel we have little influence over the food eaten at home, or the packed lunches brought in by the children in our care. However, if we learn more about 'foods for learning' ourselves, we can make suggestions, or respond to requests made by parents for help and advice. Many settings and schools offer guidance or put up posters to encourage parents to provide balanced and healthy snacks and packed lunches. Perhaps we should become more assertive about the contents of lunch boxes, and give parents guidance on how they can fill these with nutritious, yet affordable food. The internet is a good source for guidance, free, or at low cost, for settings and schools to distribute, but, as educators, we should be prepared to use our influence to ensure that during the part of the day when children are in our care, they get a nutritious diet.

At the very least, practitioners and teachers should try to have some influence over the practice in our own settings or schools, and the food we provide or sell to parents for their children. It is vital for us to discuss and agree the policy for any food and drinks provided for children in our nurseries and schools, at breakfast clubs, snack times and in school meals. Replacing white bread, refined flour cereals, jam, cheap biscuits and other

sweet foods with whole grain cereals, soup, or vegetables and dips, will prepare children for learning and keep them feeling full for longer. This will have a minimal effect on costs, but a measurable effect on how children approach learning and maintain focus.

Nutritious foods at the beginning and end of the day are important, but many children still need food 'little and often' during the day, and can't rely on crisps and chocolate bars from their lunchboxes to sustain them for the six or seven hours of the school day. Scientists and nutritionists tell us that several small meals are better than the traditional 'three meals a day', providing better levels of insulin, lowering cortisol levels, and ensuring better management of glucose levels. Glucose is the fuel for thinking, too little of it and the brain shuts down, too much can be dangerous.

There is plenty of evidence that a balanced hot meal, rather than a random snack in the middle of the school day, is beneficial to learning, closing the attainment gap between affluent and less affluent children and significantly improving the quality of learning. This has been accepted for years in many countries, and in France there is long standing guidance for a proper lunch break and 'the need for pleasant dining environments and user-friendly facilities'. The government in England will implement a free meal scheme for five to seven year olds in 2015, joining other enlightened countries such as Finland and Sweden in providing a nutritious free meal every day for every child, regardless of their family circumstances and income.

During my childhood, school meals policy concentrated on muscle and bone growth, not on brain health, and meals then were packed full of calories, fats and sugars. Thanks in part to Jamie Oliver's campaigning, school meals in England have improved, but I hope the massive proportion of children who now eat (or wolf down/pick at/swop/discard or replace) a packed lunch, will in future get something more healthy, nutritious and appealing. Some local authorities, where politicians have already seen the benefit in offering free meals for schoolchildren, have seen educational standards and attitudes to learning rise year on year.

One of the ways we can influence children's future health is by educating families, or by modelling healthy eating in our own settings, and by knowing about nutrition ourselves.

Foods that help thinking and learning

- **Complex carbohydrates**, such as whole grain breads, pasta and biscuits which supply the brain with glucose, the fuel for learning.
- **Fruit and vegetables** – at least two vegetables and two fruits a day for vitamins, fruit sugar energy, and dietary fibre.
- **Milk** – children under five should have about a pint of **whole milk** every day (semi-skimmed milk can be given once a child is two years old).
- **Milk products** such as yogurt, milk puddings, fromage frais, butter and cheese can be given as an alternative, and in addition to liquid milk.
- **Oils and fats,** such as those in butter, vegetable fats, sunflower or olive oils should be kept to manageable minimum. However, under-twos should have a diet high in fats as, among other uses, fats are converted by the body into myelin, which strengthens the links between brain cells.
- **Proteins** such as lean meat, poultry, fish (preferably the oily kind), beans and other pulses, nuts and seeds.

In order to keep the mind functioning at its best, brain cells need around twice as much energy as any other cells in your body, and they get this from the **glucose** in our food, extracted and delivered through the blood supply. Neurons can't store glucose, so they need to have it delivered in small regular packages, and carbohydrates are an ideal way of doing this. **Complex carbohydrates**, such as whole grain cereals, and **starchy foods** such as potatoes, bread, yams, rice or pasta will keep your brain cells supplied with glucose for longer, as these carbohydrates deliver the fuel in the form of glucose in regular bursts over a longer period than simple carbohydrates. **Simple carbohydrates**, such as those found in white flour and white sugar, fizzy drinks and sweets deliver their glucose in one burst, and as neurons can't store the glucose, much of it is wasted, and it's not long before you need another 'hit'.

Children also need **vitamins and minerals**, and a diet high in fresh fruit and vegetables will give them many of the vitamins they need. **Vitamin D** is not easy to provide in food, and can't be stored in the body, so it is best when manufactured by the skin in response to direct sunlight, so children do need to be out of doors for at least some of the day. Twenty minutes of sunlight will give children and adults enough vitamin D for a day, and when children are moving in and out of the sun, or the day is more cloudy, they are less likely to be burned. Sunlight through a window will not trigger the production of Vitamin D.

Water quenches thirst, does not spoil children's appetite, and does not damage teeth. The brain is 90% water, and needs to be rehydrated in order to work properly. Water should be available at all times, but children should be encouraged to drink when they are thirsty, not because they need a particular amount per day.

There is also some evidence that children are often dehydrated without realising it, and this will reduce their ability to concentrate and absorb information. One of the roles of practitioners and teachers in the early years is to help children to monitor their own bodies, to realise when they need to visit the toilet, and to check whether they are thirsty. The youngest children may need help with this, by regular reminders about both of these. Modelling drinking water yourself will also give a powerful message, and it should always be accepted practice for adults to drink water during sessions.

Other drinks offered during the day should be restricted to milk and diluted fruit juice, with the proviso that both will affect appetite for more nutritious foods.

A note for yourself – remember that coffee, tea and sugary drinks make you pee and lose even more precious liquid for your brain. So, if you want a **quick boost** yourself, try a handful of nuts, a piece of fruit or even half a banana. If you want to give the children a quick energy boost try these snacks which can all be prepared by the children.

Healthy snacks

- Small fingers of wholegrain or wholemeal toast or sliced pitta bread with some hummus or peanut butter.
- Vegetable sticks – carrot, celery, pepper – with a yogurt dip.
- A handful of raisins or grapes, or sliced bananas.
- Cheese straws or scones made with wholemeal flour.
- Halved or quartered low-sugar cereal bars (check the labels).
- Diluted, unsweetened fruit juice or fruit squash, cartons of semi-skimmed milk or unsweetened yogurt drinks.
- Fresh popcorn made without salt or sugar.
- High-fibre cereal with semi-skimmed milk.
- Unsalted nuts (check your group for allergies!) and seeds – try mixing with dried fruit.

As children get older, offering these small snacks is less common practice, but the benefits are great, and once established, schools will soon notice the difference. The excuse for having a school tuck shop with 'empty calorie' or high salt snacks and crisps, is often that it raises money for much needed extras, but a move to more healthy snacks such as those above, could make money and raise standards!

Some children are more fortunate than others, as their parents can choose whether or not to give them a healthy diet rich in the things their brains need. Other children live in families where 'food insecurity' is the norm. Food insecurity is not the same as hunger, but these families have to make hard choices between giving their children healthy foods, or cheaper, more filling, but less nutritious versions, often resulting in a diet that is inadequate in essential nutrients for normal growth and development. These families can't afford regular balanced meals, reduce the size of the meals they do have, or reduce the quality and variety of the family's diet. Food insecurity has now been found to affect the growth and development of children, particularly infants and toddlers, and, longer term, to result in lower achievement, emotional problems, and poor health. These children are likely to spend more time in hospital, and to have problems in cognitive language and behavioural development. Surprisingly, these children are also more like to become obese during their childhood, what has been described as 'simultaneously overfed and undernourished'.

Children really are what they eat, and if we want the children in our families or our settings and schools to be the best thinkers and learners they can be, then diet and nutrition are essential building blocks. We know enough about food today to make sure than even if we as adults are not eating and drinking the right things, then we should try to help children before it's too late. Healthy eating and healthy living are important parts of the curriculum, and are now included even in the earliest years of education provision. In the guidance for practitioners in England, children as young as two are to be 'supported in understanding healthy eating'; and by five, children are encouraged to 'understand and make healthy choices', and to 'eat a healthy range of foodstuffs'.

It may be that the role of schools and settings in supporting healthy eating across a whole nation is the key to future child health and lower obesity figures. However, without support for families in need, the foundation months and years between conception and starting school will continue be an undernourished desert for some children, affecting their lives and potential for learning for the rest of their lives.

Points to ponder

- Language develops differently in boys and girls. How do practitioners respond to this in settings and schools? Are there methods, resources and techniques that may help professionals to close the gap?

- In a climate where there is an over-emphasis on reading, writing, sitting still and listening, how could practitioners make sure that the skills of boys, such as climbing, running, problem solving and risk taking, are valued as highly as those developed by girls?

- When they start school, boys have spent less time talking, listening or watching each other. Do managers need to look at where the adults are during free choice sessions, where they could have an effect on language and communication by providing a model of a good communicator, as they join the active play enjoyed by most boys?

- Just as children need practice in picking up and manipulating small objects, they also need practice in eating, chewing and swallowing lumpy food. How could practitioners make sure parents know this, and help their children to cope with foods and drinks with lumps and textures?

- It is now clear that children from more affluent and well-educated families have a wider vocabulary than children brought up in poverty and deprivation. How could we counteract this effect in nurseries and the early years of school, narrowing the gap between the most advantaged children and those with less support at home?

Stage 4 Being me, being you – Danni is four and a half

'By the time they are two or three, children quite characteristically spend many of their waking hours in a world of imaginary creatures, possible universes, and assumed identities. Walk into any daycare centre and you will be surrounded by small princesses and superheroes who politely serve you non existent tea and warn you away from non existent monsters. . . . even two year olds will tell you that if an imaginary teddy is drinking imaginary tea, then if he spills it on the imaginary floor, the imaginary floor will require imaginary mopping-up.'

Alison Gopnik, professor of psychology

Before the age of four, children learn more words than they ever will again, and spend hours practising them in their play. Let's hear a four year old using her words as she negotiates life at home and at her nursery with her family and friends.

Danni's day

Danni (short for Danielle) hops down the stairs, dressed in her favourite pink fairy dress, made for her by her auntie. Pink shoes and pink socks on her feet, pink wand in her hand, pink handbag over her shoulder, and carrying their cat Daisy, who has a pink hair slide in her fur.

'You can't go to school like that, Princess Danni!' says her mum, putting down her magazine, 'And I haven't got time to wait while you choose which clothes you are going to wear. I've been ready for ages, so just put on the sweatshirt and leggings you had on yesterday. Two minutes, and I'm clearing the breakfast!'

Danni races back up the stairs, shouting, 'It's not fair!' throws her dressing-up clothes to the winds and pulls on her sweatshirt and leggings but hangs on to her pink bag. She is very hungry and knows her mum means what she says about breakfast – and if she wants some of her current favourite cereal with sliced banana, she must be quick.

As she comes down the stairs again, the argument is forgotten and she is already chattering away, asking what's in her lunch box, reminding her mum that she has promised to take her shopping after school, asking where Dad is, catching the cat to remove the pink hair slide, all while eating her cereal and without a single space for her mother to speak.

'Oh and I need a towel,' she says, 'It's for the hairdresser.'

Her mum is used to Danni's peculiar demands and quickly finds her an old towel, which Danni stuffs into her pink bag. 'Did you go to the hairdresser's on Friday? I didn't meet you and your dad never has time to stop and find out what you've been doing.'

'Yes, it was great, Mrs Green was there having her hair cut and Sandra from down the road was having eye-lights. She had loads of shiny silver paper in her hair, that's why it must be called eye-lights.'

Danni's mum, Charlotte laughs. 'Come on, put your bowl in the sink and I'll explain about 'eye-lights' in the car.'

Danni's level of language development is partly due to her lively, inquisitive nature and desire to be everybody's friend. It is also partly due to the fact that her mother has always been a reader, wanted to pass on this pleasure to her child, and has read and told stories to Danni ever since she was born. The third contributor to her early language development and reading is that Danni is a girl. Many girls are ready to start reading by the time they are four and a half, and Danni will be one of them. She is already 'reading' the books in the book corner, and recognising familiar words in the classroom. She also has good hearing, and playing sound games is one of her favourite activities. This will enable her to learn phonic skills quickly, and use them effectively in reading and writing.

Remember Mari, lip reading Eugenia's face to learn how to speak, and Sam picking up messages about language from Jan's face and body as she becomes worried about his mum, and from his chatterbox sisters. These are all examples of the ways that children begin from their first months to watch the other people in their lives, trying to make sense of this puzzling world.

Make-believe

At four and a half, Danni is in the stage of development when make-believe is very important, and it is the same for most children of her age. She has lots of experience of interesting adult and child behaviour, both in real life and in books, on TV and DVD, and she is always being someone else. She has also watched and listened to people so carefully that her body movements, expressions and even her voice are faithful copies of what she sees and hears.

One of the people Danni watches closely is her teacher. She has plenty of opportunities to watch her, so she does very good impressions of a Reception teacher reading a story or organising a class of four year olds in undressing for PE. Jeff, Danni's dad, caught her doing this in her bedroom one night, as she read a story to a group of soft toys, soundly telling them off for fidgeting, praising them for 'good sitting' and asking questions about the story, as she held the book up for the toys to see. He crept away again, but was laughing so much when he got downstairs that he could hardly speak as he told Charlotte what he had just seen.

Danni talks non-stop. She has learned so many words in four years, and they almost tumble over each other as she tries to use them. She listens carefully, but her inexperience sometimes leads to misunderstanding of new words, such as 'eye-lights' rather than highlights, or 'serving tree' for their new conservatory. She is a great leader among her friends and is always suggesting some new make-believe game, usually starting in the home corner, but often reaching out around the room to involve everyone in the room. Last week Danni and her friend Pavan started a circus play that lasted several days and every child in the class was involved at one time or another, making signs and tickets, finding costumes (lengths of fabric and string 'tails'), making masks and other props, practising tricks, and organising the audience. Paula, Danni's teacher, supports this type of play, and is prepared to adapt or even abandon her planned activities to support the thinking and learning involved in such complex play. She watched and listened to the way the children worked together, offered help when she saw the need, responded to requests for resources and space by helping to move furniture, and found stories and songs about circuses to enhance the children's work. She also provided materials for the children to write, paint and draw circus themed pictures and stories. The short project ended with a performance for the nursery children from the next-door class, which they greatly enjoyed.

Danni's language development is well ahead of the expected level for her age. Plenty of stories, parents who read, endless role-play, and singing, rhymes and rhythm work all feed her language use, providing her with an extended vocabulary and a developing sense of humour and fun in using words. At group times, Danni always has plenty to say, and sometimes her teacher has to ask her gently to let someone else have a turn. Danni's teacher would be surprised at how carefully she has been watched at these times, as Danni soaks up movements and expressions to use later in her play. Good language development needs careful listening, concentrated watching, and endless imitation.

Even as adults, we continue to imagine 'What if. . .?' as we watch actors or celebrities on the TV or in magazines, read books with powerful characters, see the winners of the lottery and imagine what we would do if we won a million. Our brains continue to use mirror neurons to reflect the activity itself, to help us imagine other lives and activities. We also copy adults we admire by getting the same clothes, haircut or make-up, buying the same car, or moving to the same part of town.

Psychologists call this activity 'counterfactual' thinking and activity, and they say that in this way, children are trying on the behaviours, actions and feelings of others, playing the 'What if . . .' game. Dressing up, play with puppets and small world characters, and pretend play with child or adult sized tea-sets, hairbrushes, high heeled shoes and other props are all examples of counterfactual play, and four year olds are masters of it.

Danni's friends

Danni's class is full of counterfactual thinkers. Their stage of development means they still need to do their thinking through movement, and whole body dressing up is their favourite way. There is Danni's friend Pavan, who spends most of his day dressed as a superhero, his current favourite counterfactual characters, Superman, Batman, Spiderman or Ben Ten. With their trademark deep colours of reds, blues, greens and black (colours which stimulate activity in the body and brain) he races around the outdoor area rescuing people, fighting baddies, and generally saving the world. If other boys have the superhero cloaks, he will play with small world superhero figures in the sand or the bricks, making towers to fly from or tunnels to hide in.

There is Paula, wheeling a baby in a toy pushchair. Handbag over her arm, and wearing a smart red coat, she walks carefully to the outside door and out into the garden, where she chats with the children playing with the wheeled toys. She takes her baby from the pram and holds it up to look at the blossom on the tree, something her key person did with her when she was a baby at the nursery next door. Paula has a new baby brother and spends as much time as she can in the home corner replaying what she sees her mum doing at home. She has grabbed one of the quieter boys to be the Dad in her 'What if?'

world, and he is trailing along behind her, not quite sure what he is supposed to be doing. The counterfactual play of boys will tend to be much more associated with action than domestic bliss, so David will probably either drift away to join a more active group, or take on an active role in the play, such as running off saying 'I'm going to the football now!'

If you watch children in any early years setting you will see that most of them are doing counterfactual thinking at some time during the day, and early years practitioners and teachers understand how important this activity is for children's learning. They use stories, familiar characters and whole-body play to help children understand new language and concepts. They will also include objects, stories and characters from popular culture to engage children in mathematical and scientific thinking, and they track children's interests in order to make a good match between the activities they offer and the interests of individuals and groups.

Hairdresser's role-play

Last week following a discussion between a group about whether a boy could be a hairdresser, Danni's teacher, Carol, took the children to visit the local hairdresser. They went in small groups, so they could see what happened in a place where many of them had never been. The hairdresser persuaded some of his clients to be watched as they had their hair shampooed, cut and dried, and the children took lots of photos during their visit. The hairdresser gave them some sample bottles of shampoo and conditioner, and some rollers, combs and brushes to take away.

During the rest of the week the children, helped by Carol and Maureen, their practitioners, set up a hairdresser's salon in their room. They moved furniture to make a corner near the sink, and collected all the things they needed – towels, empty bottles for shampoo and conditioner, brushes, combs and even some scissors (after a discussion about how these should be used). The children looked at all the photos they had taken, and saw that they needed a telephone, an appointment book, magazines and chairs for people waiting in the queue.

Boys and girls were equally interested in the visit and the preparation for the salon. The hairdresser is a man, and that was a surprise to some boys, who thought hairdressing was something for girls. One of the boys took photos of the children and adults in the setting to make a stylebook, and another took responsibility for making the signs and notices for the shop.

The hairdresser's shop has been the centre for counterfactual play, as children become stylists and customers, some even taking on the roles of their own mothers or older sisters. The salon extended its range by adding a nail bar and a special service for cutting the hair of babies, so the home corner dolls could have their hair washed and styled.

As they play in the hairdresser's salon, Danni and her friends are learning about the real world, they are beginning to use language for thinking, 'What style do you want?', 'When can you come?', 'How do you do highlights?' They are reading and writing for real purposes as they make appointments and make notices. They are using ICT as they photograph and print the pages for their stylebook. They are practising the language of numbers and money as they calculate the prices and give change. These real-life experiences help them to make sense of and internalise the more formal group activities when the teacher is in the lead. They are myelinating this learning by using the cerebral links in whole body activities, turning simple linking of cells into thinking and solving problems.

After a busy day, Danni's mum comes to meet her. Carol and Maureen know that the usual answers to 'What did you do today?' will be 'Just played', or 'Nothing'. They have tried to pre-empt this disappointing response to all their work by jotting some notes on a blackboard or running some of the photos they have taken during the day through the whiteboard. As the parents and children look back on their day, Danni's mum says, 'What were you doing here?' pointing to a photo. Danni says 'Oh, yes, now I remember in my brain – we made the hairdressers!'

The photos and reminders have triggered her memories of the day and Danni will be more likely to process these into long-term storage after a visual reminder.

Following children's interests

At Danni's school, the teachers and their teaching assistants (TAs) are encouraged to spot and nurture children's interests, and where appropriate, to adjust their own planning to incorporate these. This does not mean abdication to the children, but a careful alteration to the content of adult-led sessions to focus on the children's interests. This might include linking literacy sessions to the theme, adding music and songs, and offering creative activities linked to the current interest. Sometimes there is more than one centre of interest in progress simultaneously, carefully balancing topics planned by teachers and those initiated by groups of children. This learning style suits Danni perfectly, and, as she continues her journey towards statutory schooling, she is making good progress in all areas of learning.

See, hear, say and do – the mystery of memory

Why do children remember some things and not others? Why do some children remember what they have experienced and some remember nothing? Why does the time of day, the weather, the emotional state of the children and my enthusiasm make so much difference?

We remember things when we repeat them, and that goes for experiences too. If we revisit an experience, and particularly if we talk about it, we remember it better – with the magic of myelin and the mystery of memory.

But remembering things permanently is no good unless we can retrieve them again, and four year olds will remember, and retrieve those memories more easily if activities are:

- Relevant – with real meaning for them.
- Active – with whole-body, physical involvement.
- Stress free – enjoyable and stimulating.

This is why lack of emotional engagement, enthusiasm and interest can reduce the 'memorability' of any activity! If a child is unwell, anxious, hungry, cold or tired, their ability to learn and remember will be impaired. Another difficulty is that different parts of the brain are involved in learning (experiencing something) and remembering. A child may be involved, enthused and apparently learning, but that learning is still vulnerable, and can be destroyed by stress chemicals in the brain, or even by the next bit of incoming information.

The practitioners and teachers in Danni's school know that retrieval can be a real problem for some children, and that constant pressure from children like Danni, who always seems to know the answer, can make retrieval even more difficult. These adults know that children's response time to a question may well be as long as ten seconds, much longer than we usually give them at school or at home. A real effort is now being made in classes throughout the primary school to give children more time to respond.

It's also important to know that the journey from short-term memory to long-term memory is fraught with difficulties. A new experience or piece of learning is only held in the short-term memory for a very short time, and it can easily be pushed aside by the next impulse or stimulus before it can be processed to longer term storage. Young children live in a stimulating world, and important bits of learning can easily be over-ridden by the window-cleaner, a spider on the ceiling, or the pattern on another child's shirt. These can prove much more interesting than what an adult is saying, and can mean that the information doesn't even make it to the short-term memory.

Recall of memories

Memory has been described as the function that ties together learning, understanding and consciousness. There is no specific site in the brain where particular memories are stored, and no particular way in which they are remembered (reconstructed). However, there are three major players in the process: the amygdala, the hippocampus and the frontal cortex. Remember the amygdala and its role as a gatekeeper in emotions? In memory, the amygdala decides on the 'emotional importance' of the experience and whether to mark it as one that arouses strong emotions. The amygdala is more likely to mark negative memories as important if they arouse fear, anxiety and sadness.

Information also goes simultaneously to the hippocampus, which is central to remembering, and the cortex, which appears to package the memory into a whole experience, drawing together the senses, language and emotion associated with the memory. It's no wonder that as our brains become more complex and, particularly as we get older, the routes to memories are complex and sometimes we get lost.

Triggering recall of memories through the use of pictures, photos, objects and discussion plays an important part in processing short-term memories into long-term storage. However, one of the best tools for processing short-term memory into medium- and long-term memory is rest time and sleep. As we rest or fall into sleep, the brain has the time and capacity to organise the things that have happened during the day, moving these from short- to medium- and medium- to long-term memory. This is a complex job, and one of the reasons why children need plenty of sleep, and babies need so much more than we do. Even as adults, we need sleep to help us process the experiences we have had, and we will often find that a memory that has escaped us all day surfaces just before we go to sleep.

It is also important to give children time to process and recall during learning and after learning. In our fast-moving lifestyle, children are often rushed from experience to experience, both in school and at home, with so little processing time, and the ever-present screen playing its part in diverting the process of memory making. In Danni's school, the plenary discussion provides an opportunity for revisiting and discussing recent events and learning opportunities. These sessions are followed by opportunities to revisit the focus activity in free play, completing the memory circle, and helping to protect new memories from being pushed aside by the next experience. In this way, supported by practitioners at nursery and parents at home, Danni and her friends follow a process of do, practise, remember, recall, practise again:

- An interest arises, stimulated by the experiences of the children or a stimulus such as a visit arranged by adults.
- The children initiate counterfactual play around the focus.
- The adults observe and note this interest and support it by providing objects and other stimuli.
- The interest is promoted in adult-led activities.
- Discussion and reflection are encouraged in plenary sessions which include the use of talking partners and links with home learning.
- Photos, books and other objects of interest are displayed to encourage further memory and 'remembering'.

The Characteristics of Effective Learning (CEL)

Let's return to the CEL and look at the guidance there for the optimum environment for learning. How do the practitioners in Danni's class use the CEL to support Danni, helping her to concentrate, learn and remember?

At regular intervals, Carol and the other teachers in Nursery and Reception classes meet to look at a range of the characteristics, as well as the age related EYFS Development

Matters statements, checking these against their practice. Currently they are discussing the following ten statements from the CEL, asking the question 'Do we. . .?':

- Help children concentrate by limiting noise, and making spaces visually calm and orderly.
- Plan first-hand experiences and challenges appropriate to the development of the children.
- Provide something that is new and unusual for them to explore, especially when it is linked to their interests.
- Notice what arouses children's curiosity, looking for signs of deep involvement to identify learning that is intrinsically motivated.
- Ensure children have time and freedom to become deeply involved in activities.
- Ensure that children can maintain focus on things that interest them over a period of time. Help them to keep ideas in mind by talking over photographs of their previous activities.
- Use the language of thinking and learning: think, know, remember, forget, idea, makes sense, plan, learn, find out, confused, figure out, trying to do.
- Support children's interests over time, reminding them of previous approaches and encouraging them to make connections between their experiences.
- Give feedback and help children to review their own progress and learning. Talk with children about what they are doing, how they plan to do it, what worked well and what they would change next time.
- Plan linked experiences that follow the ideas children are really thinking about.

Carol and her TA Naomi, are also using the EYFS guidance specific to children from 40–60+ months, like Danni, to ensure that the teaching matches the needs of children at this stage of development. 'Do we. . .?':

- Set up shared experiences that children can reflect upon, e.g. visits, cooking, or stories that can be re-enacted.
- Help children to predict and order events coherently, by providing props and materials that encourage children to re-enact, using talk and action.
- Set up displays that remind children of what they have experienced, using objects, artifacts, photographs and books.
- Provide for, initiate and join in imaginative play and role-play, encouraging children to talk about what is happening and to act out the scenarios in character.
- Provide ways of preserving memories of special events, e.g. making a book, collecting photographs, tape recording, drawing and writing.

- Invite children and families with experiences of living in other countries to bring in photographs and objects from their home cultures including those from family members living in different areas of the UK and abroad.
- Provide opportunities indoors and outdoors and support the different interests of children, e.g. in role-play of a builder's yard, encourage narratives to do with building and mending.

Thinking and remembering are complex activities and they both need the same conditions – a calm and supportive atmosphere, time to practise and process experiences, sensitive adult support that does not intrude on children's interests, and plenty of hands-on, interesting activities where children can become deeply involved.

Encouraging children to remember what they are learning

In adult-led activities, the children in Danni's class will be introduced to skills for reading, writing and thinking in a slightly more formal way than in Sam's nursery class. They spend short periods every day, either in a whole group or in small groups, where the practitioners introduce planned activities that link children's current thinking and interests naturally to the next set of skills they will need.

Activities supporting the development of reading and writing skills include:

- Handling and enjoying books, by including some books about the jobs adults do, for reading in the book corner and in story sessions.
- Listening to stories and poems read by adults and children, and reading stories themselves.
- Making up their own stories and sometimes drawing or writing these in simple home-made books.
- Phonological activities (associated with understanding and listening for sounds), by singing, playing phonic games, practising rhythm and beat by clapping and using rhythm sticks, listening for the first and last letters in words, and collecting and handling objects in 'sound baskets' (a development of the treasure basket idea, where collections of objects with the same initial sound are explored and discussed).
- Writing and mark making such as using ribbon sticks to exercise muscles in arms and shoulders, picking up very small objects with tweezers or chopsticks to exercise fingers, making marks in sand or shaving foam or forming letters in play dough, talking about and writing cards and letters (including thank-you letters to the hairdresser), drawing and labelling diagrams of the things they have done or made.

Following every small group activity, the resources are available to the children for free choice, to include in their play indoors or outside, where they are sometimes transformed into mark making out of doors with water or liquid mud, flying plastic bag kites, spraying paint on a shower curtain, banging rhythms on pots and pans hung on the fence, or writing in the outdoor writing corner. In this way children can secure the skills they are learning through practice.

There is plenty of evidence that if practitioners leave the resources from one day teaching for the children to use the following day, many children will return voluntarily to repeat the activity.

The myelin switch

Many of us have wondered how children choose the activity they will start with from the many on offer in their setting. Michael Gurian, an experienced researcher into learning, maintains that many children come into our settings and classrooms ready to learn, with an often unconscious 'myelin switch' primed and ready to go. He says:

> *'In a supportive, well-led environment, the mind gravitates towards learning what it needs to learn in order to grow. The brain has, to a great extent, its own blueprint of how to grow itself, and if a classroom is set up to let the brain explore, it moves in the neural motions required.'*
>
> Michael Gurian *Boys and Girls Learn Differently* (Jossey Bass, 2010)

Any experienced practitioner in the early years will recognise that some children go straight to an activity as if drawn by a magnet, perhaps going day after day to the dressing-up box as Danni does, or the train set that is Sam's favourite. These children may use the same resources to explore and replay different experiences. Others may take longer to decide, they stand in the middle of the room, slowly circling as they look round the room for the trigger for their learning. I call it 'lighthouse behaviour'. The child may be looking for a particular child or toy, or something they were working with yesterday, and often, they don't know what they need until they see it. They may pause occasionally in this turning, as if considering whether they have found what they need. When they do see the trigger for their learning they go straight to it and often stay with this activity for long periods of time.

Understanding what is going on here really helps us in our thinking about an ideal learning environment. Many practitioners complain that some children 'never settle' or 'flit from activity to activity', often disturbing others, and the myelin switch doesn't get switched on. There are several reasons for this:

'I don't know what to choose!'

The child may be under pressure from circumstances beyond their (or your) control. These children may simply not be able to concentrate because their bodies and brains are full of cortisol, which gets in the way of thinking and learning. They may be hungry, thirsty or tired. They may just be at a stage of development when they simply can't make choices without help from an adult. This child just can't sense what the switch is telling them.

'I need it, and I can't see it!'

The child may not be able to see the activity they want – in this case, the trigger activity may be outside, in a cupboard, under a pile of other boxes or behind a very cheerful but frustrating curtain. It may even, in some settings, be down the corridor, round the corner, on the top shelf of a locked store room, where it was returned after yesterday's visit to the hairdresser's when this child was asked to be the group photographer.

'I want what you've got!'

The activity may already be in use, and the child can see that there is no place in the game for them. This situation may well lead to frustration as the child tries to find an alternative to their first choice, and some practitioners now separate resources such as Lego into several smaller baskets or boxes so there are opportunities for several children to use the same resource.

'I can't reach it!'

The toy or game may be difficult to access. Sometimes a child will want to use the bucket that is at the back of the outdoor shed, the puzzle at the bottom of the pile, or on a top shelf, visible but unattainable. The problems associated with getting this resource may be more than the child can cope with and they pass on to something else.

'It's broken!'

The thing they want to use may be broken or have missing pieces. There is nothing more frustrating than completing most of a puzzle, only to find that the last piece is missing. Children deserve the best we can provide, and we should make sure that shelves and boxes are checked regularly and broken or damaged books and resources are removed. It is better to have a smaller range of good quality resources than a great pile of sub-standard, frustrating stuff.

'It's gone!'

The activity the child enjoyed yesterday, and would love to do again today has been carefully tidied away.

If the child cannot see or access what they want, or if their desired tool for learning is not available, they will drift, and may become a distraction to other children's learning as they try to cope with a learning switch that is primed but can't be switched on. Experienced practitioners and teachers watch carefully and intervene to support individuals, and this may mean reorganising their resources so the children can see everything, walking round the room with a child to look with them at the resources as they make their choice, or making a photo book of all the equipment, so the child can sit quietly and look for their 'thing of the moment'. This last solution is often helpful for practitioners and children in 'pack-away' settings where it may not be possible to have everything on display every day.

How are Danni and her friends doing?

If we check any list of CEL environments against the practice in Danni's life, we will see that her teacher and her parents are giving her a very good basis for future success. It is important to be tolerant of children's obsessions, their counterfactual and schema play, their need to try on the behaviours and props of adults and children they see.

Danni's mum is a very good model for parenting. She listens to her, treating Danni as an equal in conversations, while maintaining clear boundaries for behaviour and relationships. Having parents who enjoy reading and carry on learning throughout their lives, is a real bonus as Danni learns to read, write, count and become an independent learner herself.

The environment for learning at school is carefully constructed to encourage children to explore, experiment and extend their learning, while providing regular support through interventions planned to respond to children's needs and interests. Provision for the classes for three to five year olds follow the guidance for effective learning, and the classes for older children build on this methodology by spending time teaching thinking skills.

By the time Danni reaches the end of this school year, she will be ready to continue her learning in a new class. She will then be 'statutory school age' and will embark on the National Curriculum for Key Stage 1, with a classroom and programme very similar to that in the early years, where the curriculum is built on a thematic approach which responds to children's interests, continues to extend and expand skills in interesting and vibrant lessons led by teachers, and gives time for children to consolidate their learning in 'continuous provision'.

A message from Danni

I *love* being other people, and role-play is an essential part of every day for me, and all my friends! We get obsessed with things and spend all day (and sometimes all evening) exploring them. Then we need all sorts of stuff to make costumes and props for our play. I'm really glad that our parents and teachers help us to find what we need. Most of us are getting better at sitting still on the carpet, but sometimes it's hard when we can see the things we want to play with, when we are doing phonics or Big Write. Sometimes I am looking so hard at our how Mrs Starner is sitting, talking and moving, that I don't hear what she is saying, and I get told off for not listening.

Practitioners

- Children need plenty of time for make-believe play as they practise the things they see adults doing. The objects and clothing used by these fascinating adults are also important to every child, and should be as open-ended as possible, so they can use them in different ways and create different real-life stories. How could you make these resources available and easily accessible?

- Children are always watching you, and in general, boys are more interested in watching men, while girls will often watch women. We need strong, sensitive models of what men do and how they behave at work and at home. How should practitioners and teachers provide models of both men and women, so children have the widest possible range of how men and women work and behave?

- Once children are playing in role, it is sometimes very difficult to stop, and this may trigger 'chimp' behaviour. How should practitioners balance the pressures of the programme and the curriculum and the need to transition from one activity to another?

Parents

- Children need time to finish what they are doing before changing to something else. Try to give them plenty of warning when change is about to happen.

- At this age and stage of development, children often become obsessed with adults and children they see every day, in real life or on TV. They will copy the behaviour or language they see or hear, and sometimes this may surprise or even shock you as they try out what they see adults or other children doing or saying. Try to be understanding when this happens, but it doesn't mean you have to accept this behaviour without comment. Be clear about what you expect of your child, and what is unacceptable in language or behaviour in your family.

Interlude 4 I don't need you, but please don't go! The debate about continous and enhanced provision

'Children who are allowed to play freely will demonstrate a genius for lateral thinking and problem solving of which we adults should be envious. All too often . . ., well-intentioned adults are too quick to intervene . . ., and on both sides important possibilities remain unrealised.'

Martin Rawson and Michael Rose, education writers

Most children begin to display independent behaviour when they are between two and three years old, and this age is sometimes described as the 'terrible twos' when tantrums and other defiant confrontations are common. During this stage, children are beginning to see themselves as separate beings from their mothers, testing out the boundaries of behaviour, while maintaining strong links with their key care-givers. This sense of independence becomes more permanent as children grow older, and some of their most memorable and permanent learning experiences are 'self-initiated', either alone or in the company of other children. 'Counterfactual thinking' in role-play and while using familiar toys and equipment found in early years settings – small world, puppets, construction, and particularly resources for playing in role – is at the heart of these independent activities. Children use these materials to explore relationships, to communicate with others, to try on behaviours and to learn about the world in which they live.

When talking about the optimum learning conditions for children before seven years of age, there is a long-standing and continuing debate about the amount of physically present help and guidance children should receive from adults. Adults can be a great support for learning, but they can also be an inhibitor, once described as 'stamping all over children's activities with their size nine boots', often restricting children's learning to the achievement of narrow and simplistic objectives owned by the adult.

We can all recognise 'teaching' or 'adult-led activity' when we see it: an adult working closely with individuals, groups or the whole class, controlling the activity closely, talking a lot, demonstrating, managing. The children are usually sitting down for most of the time, who talks and when is carefully managed, and the session often results in written outcomes.

We accept that children need to learn to sit still, listen and write things down, but it is also well understood that such adult-led activity is not enough for young learners who need to find out things for themselves, to be active and to play. Play, including counterfactual thinking, is the way young children build their brains and find out about the world. In play, children really show us what they know and what currently interests them. This time for play and exploration, provides opportunities when the child selects, organises and follows their own learning; adults set up an environment for investigative play, and then step back, watch, and join in when invited.

Somewhere between these two extremes – adults in the lead, or children in the lead – is a situation where adults and children work together as equals, learning together, and expanding the environment by extending the resources as their conversations and thinking develop. This magical balance of 'enough, but not too much' adult intervention is often described as 'continuous and enhanced provision' and I will attempt here to describe the subtle differences between child-led play and adult direction, which are really on a continuum from complete freedom to complete control.

I have chosen to describe and explore the range of early years play situations currently provided as follows, starting with the lowest possible level of adult intervention:

1. **Completely free play** – the childhood idyll

2. **Continuous provision** – totally led by the children themselves

3. **Enhanced provision** – play enhanced by the addition of resources, usually selected by the adults

4. **Extended provision** – play enhanced by challenges and provocations presented by the adults

5. **The teacher as leader** – adult-led activities

1. Completely free play – the childhood idyll

An example of complete freedom is a group of children of mixed ages, playing in a garden in the evening, without adults. They choose what they are going to do, what they will use, and where they will play. Their games flow easily all over the garden and into the field beyond. The group splits and reforms, at one point leaving just one child absorbed in watching a worm, and at another, organising an informal game of football. Individuals in the group collect some things to make a den – sticks, an old sheet, a bit of carpet from the shed. They light a small fire and try to cook some potatoes and apples from the garden. Resources available include stones, sticks, logs, mud, water, matches, leaves, and anything else they find, combined and recombined in endless variation as the weather and seasons change. No adult is present, and the children are completely free to use and do what they please. An adult may appear to provide a snack, a plaster or a message from another parent, but these intrusions have little impact on the play.

Despite the restrictions of health and safety guidance, this sort of play, which many of us remember from our childhoods, is still possible in the world outside the education system. Children still play in groups of mixed ages and use the resources offered in the local environment. They are unsupervised and cope with risks. When arguments arise, they sort them out in the group, and grazed knees, lost gloves, dirtied clothes and muddy hands are commonplace. The children go home when it gets dark.

Although we now worry far more about 'free range' play, and sometimes restrict it in the name of safety, it is still possible for children to have this sort of freedom in out-of-school time. However, it is less common to find such play situations in nurseries and schools, apart from some in Scandinavia where mixed ages play and learn together, and in schools where a philosophy of free play is at the heart of their curriculum, but this sort of play is rare in schools funded by the state. During the second half of the twentieth century, as early years provision became more widespread, and much of it was under state or local community control, written curriculum documentation became common. Guidance on objectives and outcomes was written down and often inspected for quality. The effect of writing a curriculum down seems inevitably to result in less freedom, and more adult control, even when objectives include the need for children to play and become more independent. 'Play' almost became a subject of the curriculum, defined, quantified and measured in much the same way as history or English.

2. Continuous provision, always there!

Once children are cared for outside their own home, a range of constraints comes into play. Practitioners are 'in loco parentis', substitute adults with all the responsibilities that entails. Children are not allowed to play totally unsupervised, and risks are carefully managed.

The nearest to this complete freedom comes when children have time to choose their own resources from a range on offer in the nursery or classroom. These resources are wide-ranging, but not infinite in their variety, and there are rules about how, where and what the children can do with them. In the most imaginative and enabling of environments, they are as near as possible to the freedom described above, but the adults are always within reach, carefully supervising, even if actually out of sight.

Free play, child-initiated learning, free-flow, child choice, 'over to you', are some of the terms used to describe this provision (at a childminder's, nursery, daycare or school) where adults provide the conditions and resources for learning and exploration, and the children engage freely with these, choosing what and who they will play with, where they will play, and for how long. Adults are just another resource, available to the children, interacting if invited, but not taking over the play.

Sometimes practitioners will articulate, or even write down in their planning, some general objectives or intentions for this sort of play. These intentions will usually be the overarching ones that all practitioners understand, but sometimes forget to articulate, even to each other. In Danni's nursery, the practitioners realise that parents (and others who visit the setting) may not be familiar with early learning, so they have agreed the intentions for child-initiated learning, which they have displayed on the Parents' noticeboard, and offer to parents as part of the visiting programme before their child starts at the nursery (see poster on p. 112). In this way, the practitioners share their intentions for play, ensuring that parents value it as much as the practitioners do.

It is now well understood that in the activities that they select themselves, children will be building and strengthening links in their brains through the repetitive play referred to as schemas, and until we understand why children do these things, they can be extremely annoying. A child who persists in choosing the same thing to play with every day is sometimes a worry for practitioners or parents, and they try to prise or tempt the child away from their current favourite. However this repetitive play is absolutely essential for children. In this play they are literally changing the architecture of their growing brains.

Sometimes a child will enter the setting knowing exactly what they want to do – they want to finish the construction they started the day before, or play that game again with their friend, or get out the jungle animals to play out the film they saw the previous night on TV. However, it seems that sometimes the child does not consciously know, or is not able to articulate what their brain needs to practise until their 'myelination switch' is thrown by seeing a toy, a friend, or an activity.

What is your child doing when they are playing?

Sometimes you will think your child is **'JUST PLAYING'** but really they are doing more than that! They are:

- Making friends and playing with other children.
- Becoming independent and making choices.
- Choosing what they will play with, or where they will play.
- Exercising their bodies and brains in indoor and outdoor play.
- Experiencing play in all weathers and seasons.
- Playing with new objects and resources such as dough, clay, paint, sand, water, mud and bricks.
- Exercising the links in their brains and growing more.

And they are:

- Learning to share and take turns.
- Learning to look after toys and put them away.
- Learning how things work.
- Learning new skills for using tools and equipment, such as gardening and woodwork tools, glue, scissors, staplers, computers, simple musical instruments.
- Learning about reading and writing by reading books, telling stories, using puppets and singing songs.
- Learning about others through role-play and dressing up.

During this time, we will be keeping your children safe, supporting their learning, not telling them what to do, but helping them to do what they choose.

The resources for this sort of self-initiated and repetitive play, often called continuous provision, will be the backdrop to every setting and very familiar to early years practitioners.

At home, children love to play with empty cardboard boxes, kitchen equipment, plates and cutlery, clothes pegs, or even their parents' clothing or shoes. In early years settings, the practitioners provide versions of these 'open-ended' or 'loose parts' playthings, and in this way they can make sense of the things they see their families do, copying them to gain understanding of their purpose, the skills needed to manipulate the objects, and the social behaviours associated with them. You have only to see a child unpacking tins from a food cupboard, wrapping their teddy in a tea towel and feeding him with a plastic spoon, tottering on their mothers' high-heeled shoes, or using a plastic plate as a steering wheel, to begin to understand the learning process in action.

As young children begin to attend daycare, nursery, or the early years of school, these objects from home should still be available for them in continuous provision, to replay their experiences, as Danni and her friends do in their counterfactual play – 'What if I was a hairdresser?'.

In addition to these domestic experiences will be the classics of 'continuous provision' – the resources that form the backdrop for early learning. These are sometimes, but not always available to children in their 'out of setting play' where play with mud and grass clippings, cones and pebbles are not considered proper playthings by parents.

These constants will include:

- **Natural and malleable materials** – to expand creativity and strengthen hands and fingers – sand, water, clay, dough and other malleable materials, with cutters and other safe tools. These will feed the children's need for squeezing, rolling, pressing and cutting shapes, making food and other objects. Natural objects – fir cones, seeds, shells, twigs, pebbles and man-made objects – screws, washers, lolly sticks, reels, coins, keys etc extend this play. Of course, some children are able to reinforce these experiences at home or on walks with their families.

- **Resources for building and construction** – bricks, construction sets, tyres, logs and planks, open-ended and recycled materials such as cartons, tubes, guttering, cones, and other containers. These will be used to make and disassemble models, buildings and scenes for small world play. Joining, separating and containing schemas are often at the heart of construction, as children make and knock down bricks, join and break apart Lego, and construct dens and shelters out of doors.

- **Wheeled toys for riding, pulling pushing, climbing, swinging, jumping** – these toys, as well as providing vigorous exercise for muscles, exercise the imagination as children take on roles of adults. They can also be used in combination with open-ended resources such as crates, tubes, reels, log slices and other large items to make constructions on a larger scale.

- **Small world collections** – wheeled vehicles, animals, people from real life and stories. These are used to reconstruct experiences and stories, both familiar and fuelled by what children see on DVD and TV.

- **Creative materials and tools** – paint, crayons, markers, chalk, paper, card, pens and pencils, scissors, rulers, hole punches and staplers. These give children experience in making pictures, models, letters, cards, and other creations and representations of the things they are learning about.

- **Books and stories** – a range of simple and more complex books, fiction, non-fiction, poetry and rhymes. A wide but frequently changing collection of good quality books suitable for the age, stage of development and interests of the children, which depict and describe children like them as well as imagined characters and places.

- **Role-play resources** – both indoors and outside, for home play, imaginative and creative play, will enable children to play out the stories they make up, as well as helping them to understand the world they experience.

- **Puppets and soft toys** – simple characters to use for learning, looking after and storytelling. These companions take on roles in children's stories and thinking support imagination and creativity as they assume a life of their own.

- **Gardening, woodwork and technology tools** – for exploring the world, growing things keeping pets or minibeasts, watching the weather or the local birdlife, going on expeditions and explorations in the garden or beyond, all keep children in touch with the natural world. Insect boxes, magnifiers, real but child-sized garden and woodwork tools help children to grow and make real things, offering experiences that are not possible with make-believe, plastic tool kits.

These resources are always present, they may change slightly over time, with the age and stage of development of the children, but they are permanent. Add to these the support of sensitive adults, and you have a powerful potential for independent learning.

This tapestry of child-initiated learning in continuous provision should continue for part of every day in the early years, giving opportunities to practise new skills and reinforce new experiences.

3. Enhanced provision play enhanced by the addition of resources, usually selected by adults

Once an adult changes one of the resources in continuous provision by adding something to it, it becomes 'enhanced' – made more interesting, more of a 'fascination trap' for the children. At its simplest level, enhanced provision might look something like this:

- Food colouring, glitter or aromatherapy oils added to the plain dough.
- A box of small world people in the block area.
- A vase of flowers in the creative area, with some autumn leaves underneath.
- Some superhero writing paper in the writing corner.
- A piece of blue velvet over the chair in the book corner.
- A sign in the garden saying 'Please park here'.
- Some baby clothes in the home corner.
- A story box with figures and objects to play out a favourite story.
- A book about ants, and some magnifying glasses.

We enhance provision for many reasons, some of which might be:

- The children show an interest in something, and we want to encourage this interest.
- The activity isn't as popular as it once was and needs a boost.
- We don't see any boys (or any girls) in the activity, and want to attract them.
- A child or group requests something, to support their learning.
- We see and buy something small and attractive in a factory, charity or junk shop that we think will enhance our setting or classroom.
- We see a good idea in a magazine, on the internet, at a course or in a colleague's room.

Enhancing provision in this way is a familiar, simple and quick activity for practitioners, although we don't always think as creatively about all areas of provision as we do about our personal favourites. It doesn't change our initial intentions for continuous provision, it just refreshes it and hopefully re-kindles the children's interest.

Another reason for enhancing continuous provision is to incorporate it in a current interest. Here are some examples:

- Adding new resources, or familiar resources offered in an innovative way – a puppet left in a tree outside, with a message.
- Altering the range of resources to include some from other areas in the room – some play people in the sand tray, a pulley and a bucket on the climbing frame.
- Providing new or additional resources such as role-play clothing, books or objects to meet the interests shown by individuals or groups – some simple tabards for the Garden Centre shop.
- Rearranging the room to make a new area of interest inspired by a visit or visitor.
- Providing adult support by joining a group to extend their thinking, concentration and learning.

- Adding plastic tubing, funnels, pipettes, squeezy bottles and other containers to the water tray, following up on an observation where a group of children were using construction straws to make bubbly water.

- After a few days when sand was found everywhere and no one would admit to being responsible, the adults hid the clean bones of a turkey in the sand to restore interest in digging.

- Following up a visit to the zoo by leaving a piece of carpet and some thick markers for the children to make a map of the zoo.

- Enhancing a story by putting an explorers' bag in the role-play area, after reading *We're Going on a Bear Hunt*.

- Providing additional materials to make little story books for the retelling of *The Gruffalo* or another story, after observing and talking with a group of interested children.

- Offering shoe boxes and wallpaper or fabric scraps for children to make models of their bedrooms as part of a topic on day and night.

These enhancements are offers and the adults are not upset, offended or insistent if children don't take the offer, choosing to do sweep their offer aside and do something else instead.

4. Enhanced provision play enhanced by challenges and provocations presented by the adults

As children grow older and more mature, the enhancements may turn into specific challenges, activities which make an overt link between continuous provision and other parts of the curriculum, or extend children's use of and learning from continuous provision resources. This has been described as 'adding starch' to a familiar activity.

As these challenges are provided the practitioner/teacher talks them through and expects that most, if not all, the children in the group will attempt the challenge. Many of these challenges continue to be based on the activities available in continuous provision, but enhanced in a way that makes them more appropriate to the age of the children. Others may require the children to find, make or collect other resources, or learn to use new ones. Examples of these 'starched activities' might be:

- To give additional practice in the objectives taught during the week, in literacy: Choose a character from the box, and make up a story about them that takes them to another country. Write the beginning and the end of your story. Mathematics: Use this box of buttons to make seven different repeating patterns. Choose a way to record what you have done.

- To encourage the children to gather information relevant to a topic: Use the library or the internet to find out all you can about why leaves fall off the trees in autumn. Draw some pictures of autumn leaves, or collect some real ones, and use them to make a picture. Mrs Wallace will help you on the computer.

- To use familiar resources in new ways: Work with a friend to make the longest bridge you can. You can use bricks and any other resources. Photograph and measure your bridge and add your information to the Bridges Book.

- To give children independent experiences linked to an area of learning or subject of the curriculum: Can you make a Spring basket using recycled materials? Plan your project, collect the resources and make your basket. You need a basket each by Friday morning.

The adults may direct the children to the challenges at a particular time, or may tell the children that they can attempt the challenge at any time during the periods when they are free to work in continuous and enhanced provision. In this case, children are responsible for managing their time to ensure that they do the challenge(s) in the time they have available.

Enhancing the continuous provision with additional resources, ideas and challenges, will take the learning further than children might if left on their own. Some of these enhancements will be provided simply by an adult's presence, gently guiding the children's

thinking through suggestions and conversation. At its best, such guidance will produce sustained shared thinking, which has been described as:

> *'... an episode in which two or more individuals work together in an intellectual way to solve a problem, clarify a concept, evaluate activities, extend a narrative etc. Both parties must contribute to the thinking and it must develop and extend.'*

Iram Siraj-Blatchford

Sustained shared thinking can take place between children and adults or between children themselves, but the key element is the development and extension of talking and thinking, and thus of learning.

The provision of new resources, equipment, visits or visitors, particularly those relevant to the current thinking and interests of the children, or to topics or themes chosen by them for investigation, are other ways of promoting sustained shared thinking. Most enhanced provision takes familiar activities and resources, such as those described above, and extends them by the enhancement, although good practitioners will realise that sometimes the children will not be inspired to engage with the enhancement they have carefully provided.

The practitioners in Danni's nursery watched the interest of a group of children in the role-play area grow into an argument about whether hair and nail treatment in their 'Beauty parlour' could be done by boys. One of the practitioners heard a conversation between two groups of children, one group saying, 'Boys can't do hairdressing! You can't play, it's only for girls, isn't it Mrs Starner?'

Carol, the practitioner, was tempted to intervene and stop the play with the usual mantra agreed in the nursery that, 'You can't say "You can't play"'. However, she had another idea and said, 'I'm not sure about that. How could we find out?'

The children came up with several suggestions, one of which was to ask a hairdresser. So that's what they arranged to do, with the result that both boys and girls now feel free to play in the new hairdressing salon they have made in their role-play area.

Continuous and enhanced provision – getting the balance right

The balance of continuous and enhanced provision is currently the subject of enthusiastic debate among practitioners and teachers in many countries, as they try to resist the influences of over-regulation and inspection, and an ever increasing pressure to over-intervene in children's independent learning.

The most practical guidance will be to observe the children, as Carol did, watching to see how intense their interest already is in the continuous provision within the setting or classroom, or whether their thinking and learning would benefit by the addition of new resources, new experiences or the company of an adult. Of course, even experienced practitioners make mistakes, as did my good friend Ros Bayley, when she thought a bit of Sustained Shared Thinking (SST) would be good for the children in a home corner in her nursery. The children however had different ideas, and as she arrived, they not only left the home corner themselves, but took some of the furniture with them to set up elsewhere in the room!

5. The teacher as leader

As children become more familiar with using resources from continuous provision, the adults can decide to have more influence over some of the activities. This will involve them in observing the children to find out their current interests, using these to locate appropriate intentions within the curriculum documentation, and, using these two links, identifying appropriate activities to both interest the children and work towards curriculum objectives. Adults can then organise and resource these activities, leading them in a way that enables children to reach objectives identified by the adults.

Gradually, as the children move towards the age of about seven, teacher-led activities will gradually take up a larger proportion of the day.

Trying to quantify the proportions of the session or day devoted to each of these types of provision, inevitably leads to discussions of the nature of play in education (as opposed to play outside education). A tension now exists around how much time children should spend leading and directing their own play, with or without the direct intervention of adults.

There is no national or international agreement about what proportion of a child's time in the early years should be spent in leading their own learning. This is surprising as one of the overarching aims of education has always been to turn out independent learners who can think for themselves, and the best way to support this is in continuous and enhanced provision. However, the guidance in most countries is that whatever individual schools and settings agree about the proportion of time allocated to active, child-led learning, the balance of child-initiated (child choice activities in high quality continuous provision) and adult-led activities (enhancing or otherwise altering the provision by adult intervention) should gradually move towards more adult-led activities as the child gets older, and particularly as they reach statutory school age.

This is understandable, because children are able to cope with intervention more easily as they master the learning skills they need. However, if we look closely at a child's day, and for how much of it he or she can 'throw the myelin switch' and initiate their own learning, we may begin to understand how frustrating the day must be for many children. Even in countries such as those in Scandinavia or in New Zealand, in 'free-flow' situations in the UK, or High/Scope schools in the USA, where practitioners follow the interests of the children, the day is shaped and controlled to a great extent by adults, and children have limited times when they are able to play, free from the influence of the adults.

Think about the baby or toddler at home with a caring parent. She is usually near her mum or another carer, but free to crawl, creep and pull herself to her feet, to explore her surroundings and their contents with few restrictions. Food and drink are provided on demand, waking and sleeping happen naturally, even if this involves being carried gently from the place where she falls asleep on the floor. Even outings are planned with her needs in mind, and her programme is to a great extent the controller of the day.

Once she goes to daycare, things are different! She is woken at a time suited to her mother's work routine, even if this means going to nursery in her pyjamas. Breakfast is eaten in a rush, then into the car-seat and off to the nursery where the rest of her day must accommodate the needs of the other children, and specially the adults. Changing, snack, lunch, time with an adult, free play, nap, outdoor time, all fall into a more rigid routine or programme, imposed for the safety and convenience of the many, but with few adjustments to the individual. Is it any wonder that babies and young children find this difficult to adjust to?

Danni, at four, has a timetable even more constrained by 'institutional' rather than 'individual' needs than any babies. I lay no blame here. Few settings, even the best childminding, cannot replicate the situation in the child's own home, however hard the practitioner tries. But as pressures on mothers to go back to work earlier and earlier, ever younger babies become used to a programme where they have little control over their own play and learning, and at worst become small institutionalised parcels, carried from place to place with little concern for anything other than their physical well-being.

Although the reasons for (and some of the consequences of) this practice are well known and understood, I hope we don't live to regret the situation where financial circumstances over-ride the needs of very young children. We are already finding that although high quality early daycare can result in higher cognitive outcomes in later life, there is some evidence that long hours of daycare can result in social problems for very young children, particularly in boys. These problem behaviours sometimes emerged in mid-adolescence (at 15), more than a decade after the children had made the transition from child-care to school.

On a personal note, I was a working mother when my children were in their early years. During the desperate shortage of teachers in the 1960s, when child-care was not widely available, my son came with me into the classroom in his pram, as I did a part-time job with 40 Reception children. My son was welcomed by the children, who became 40 'brothers and sisters', leaning over the edge of his pram with objects, words, nursery rhymes and laughter. However, his day had to be governed by the school timetable, he was constrained in his pram, and once he became mobile, I had to give up the job. Four years later, by the time my daughter was born, I had moved to a new area, teacher pay and recruitment had both improved, and my daughter spent her time with a wonderfully warm, but untrained childminder. She played in the garden, went for walks and shopping locally, and generally had a normal childhood, but with three parents. Her timetable was governed by my need to be at school, and sometimes, like Sam in this book, she was ready for me before I was able to be ready to come home for her. Both my children benefitted from their early experiences, spending much of their time in self-initiated activities, but at some cost to their freedom. It was also fortunate that as a teacher, I had long holidays when we could spend time together as a family.

The constraints on children's freedom continue as they reach school age. Most written guidance advises that children should spend at least some of their time in 'child-initiated' activity but this guidance is interpreted in different ways by different practitioners. Some would expect a five year old to be following their own plans for up to half of the day, others allow much less.

Consider the disruption to Matthew's routine. He is five years old, lives in England, where he is now of statutory school age, and his day goes something like this:

Matthew's day

7:00	Matthew wakes and starts to build a model with his Lego
7:15	He is called to get dressed, have breakfast
7:30	He leaves for school
7:45 – 8:45	At breakfast club
9:00 – 9:15	Class registration
9:15 – 9:35	Phonics session
9:35 – 9:55	Introduction to the day's activities
9:55 – 10:10	Whole class discussion of current literacy topic
10:10–10:40	*Continuous/enhanced provision – one enhanced activity (craft), then a child choice activity (bricks) – 30 minutes*
10:40 – 10:45	Packing up
10:45 – 11:05	Snack and break
11:05 – 11:45	Maths activity, whole class, then group work with TA (two other groups in continuous provision)
11:45 – 12:05	Plenary
12:05 – 1:15	Dinner time
1:15 – 1:30	Introduction to afternoon activities, whole class
1:30 – 2:00	Matthew joins a group with teacher for topic work
2:00 – 2:30	*Continuous/enhanced provision (literacy focus) – 30 minutes*
2:30 – 3:00	PE
3:00 – 3:15	Story and singing
3:15 – 5:00	After school club

During the school day, Matthew spent 1 hour 30 minutes in 'continuous and enhanced provision', but only 45 minutes of this was time when Matthew could following his own ideas.

Matthew spent nearly four hours in activities directed or initiated by an adult.

If Matthew lived in Norway, Ireland, Italy, Germany or a number of other European countries, he would be free to follow his own programme for much more of the day, at least until he was six, and in Finland, Sweden and Poland, he would not attend formal school until the age of seven.

Employers and evaluators of the benefits of education systems agree that there are key abilities that will ensure a successful life after school. These are the abilities to:

- solve problems
- discuss rationally
- work well in groups.

Children who have a good balance of the five different levels of provision described above, with a gradual addition of 'starch' in the form of challenges and adult intervention should become more successful adults and more worthwhile employees than those who have experienced an overwhelmingly adult directed curriculum, particularly in their early years.

I hope we haven't risked the futures of generations of young children by curtailing their early freedom to choose their preferred learning activities and styles.

Points to ponder

- Children still need play, right up to their teenage years, and often beyond. We still play as adults, particularly when we are relaxed and interested. Given external pressures, how do practitioners and teachers make time for children to make the most of continuous and enhanced provision?
- As they get older, children can cope with more adult intervention (or interference), but they still need time for free play with all the resources in the room. This should not be just at formal breaks and lunchtimes, when their current interests may be locked in the classroom while they are banished to the cold playground. How can we preserve time for free play, while making time for activities led or supported by adults?
- Children's play is enhanced when the adults join them, but without taking over. What are the best ways of joining a group of children in their play?
- How can practitioners help parents to understand the importance of 'play with a purpose' in the early years at school?
- What is the balance of the different types of continuous and enhanced provision in your setting? Too much child-led play can be just as perilous as too much adult-directed activity. How do settings and schools achieve an appropriate balance?

Stage 5 Over the border – Eli is five and a half

'Research has shown that, probably by the age of three, and, almost certainly by the age of five, the life chances of children have generally been decided.'

Frank Field MP

During the year between five and six, children in most countries begin to attend school, and experience a formal curriculum, often with tests and assessments. Statutory school age, although it does differ between countries, is almost always accompanied by a change in the approaches to teaching and learning. Sometimes this change is well understood and guidance is continuous and helpful to the adults working both sides of the transition. The teachers continue the organisation of the curriculum and the learning environment, so that children are supported through the transition, only gradually introducing increased formality as children are ready for it.

In other countries, where there is less discussion across the transition, dislocation can happen. This can result in the introduction of pressure and formality to the curriculum before children are ready.

One of the most worrying situations is where the written curriculum documentation supports continuity, but external pressure results in moving children too fast and too young into formality. This is particularly a danger when testing, inspection and league tables of results combine to change the balance of what purports to be a curriculum based on the most recent research into child development. This next story is a description of a school where the teachers are determined to do the best for the children in their care.

Eli's story

Eli is five and a half. He is one of the 3.5 million children in England who at the time of writing are living in families in poverty. He is also one of the 65% of these children who are in poverty despite having one or both parents in work.

Families living in severe poverty:

- have nothing set aside for emergencies
- cannot replace broken electrical goods or furniture

- can't afford their children's school uniforms, or the cost of school trips
- have no spare money for holidays, hobbies or leisure activities
- can't afford to keep their homes warm
- can't afford social activities.

(Save The Children Fund, 2013)

Eli is just entering Year 1, the first year of the formal curriculum in England.

Eli cries. He cries enormous tears that roll down his cheeks like a waterfall, and those tears are not the normal tears of the beginning of term. As a Year 1 class teacher Ros is used to children's tears. Every September some of the children cry when they move from Reception, leaving the safety of familiar practitioners and a comfortable, stimulating and child-centred environment for learning. Many of them have been in the nursery for as long as they can remember.

But this is different. This small skinny boy cries silently, hopelessly, as if he understands that there is no real point in crying, even though he can't actually control the tears. School for him is something alien, despite the friendly faces and exciting activities on offer. The only things Eli knows about school are when his mum says, 'They'll mek yer talk when yer get there! And they'll mek yer stick up for yerself.'

Eli hasn't been to school and he hasn't even been to nursery or anywhere else in the huge range of childcare settings in the area. He is one of the forgotten ones – his mum, Tracey, has always lived with her mum, who lives on benefit allowances and has never worked. She loves Eli in her own way, but her own upbringing in a poor, harsh environment has limited her understanding of what children need. She does keep Eli reasonably clean, and when he was a baby, Tracey and her mum treated him like a doll. However, as we know, dolls don't grow up, but babies turn into toddlers who are much less easy to manage.

Eli's gran has looked after him since Tracey got a job, and the two women have never 'got it together' to take Eli to the local Children's Centre, even though he could have had a free full-time place. Every time their social worker tried to get them motivated, they promised, but never turned up. The problem was, Tracey has a part-time job and a bit of a difficult relationship with cider!

Eli is a quiet child, no trouble to anyone, fading into the background and fitting into his grandma's activities. His life would have stayed like this, but two things happened. One was that the social worker said that Tracey would be taken to court if Eli didn't go to school when he was five. The other was that Tracey found another man and quickly became pregnant again. The new baby took everyone's attention, Eli was a nuisance, and they wanted him out of the way.

'For goodness sake Eli, will you cut it out?' shouts Tracey, and she whips out a piece of kitchen roll, rubbing it harshly around the little boy's face. He still makes no noise but the tears do slow down a bit.

It's the first day of the new school year and it looks as if Eli is going to take quite a bit of settling. Ros approaches his mother.

'Hello Mrs. Bentley,' Ros says cheerfully. 'Please don't worry about Eli crying, I'm sure he'll be fine as soon as he gets stuck into things, and you can stay with him for as long as you like you know. There are some more mums and dads here this morning helping their children settle in.'

'I ain't got time to stay 'ere. I've got to be in work by half past nine,' declares Eli's mum. 'No, he'll be alright, take no notice of 'im, he always snivels when he don't wanna do something.'

As Tracey leaves, Ros expects Eli to rush after her, banging on the window or pulling at the door – but not Eli. He simply stands, rooted to the spot staring into space, his face expressionless. Ros walks over and puts her arm around him.

'Hello Eli,' she says softly. 'It's always scary when you go somewhere new isn't it, but it's lovely to have you here. Would you like me to show you around the classroom? There are loads of great things to play with.' Eli raises his head and looks around the room, seemingly dazed by the wide range of activities on offer. He has large, deep blue eyes that look as if they should belong to someone much older. As he gazes, Ros wonders if he might know any of the other children, but no one comes to greet him, as they would a familiar child.

However, in the bustle of the busy classroom, help is at hand! Bossy but likeable Amy has noticed Eli, and offers to play, even though she has never met him before.

'He's upset isn't he. What's 'is name?'

'He's called Eli,' Ros says encouragingly, in the hope that Amy might have more luck with him than she was having. Amy bends down and looks Eli straight in the eye.

'D'you want to play with me? Me and Keira's playing in the 'ome corner and we need someone to be the dad. D'you wanna be the dad Eli?'

To Ros's amazement, Eli nods. Amy clasps him by the hand and leads him off to the home corner with such speed that his feet barely touch the floor. Once there, he sits in a chair and takes on his role, the quietest dad they've had in the home corner for a long while.

After circulating around the classroom where the children and some of their parents are playing with puzzles, bricks, sand and paint, Ros checks on the home corner. Amy is soon at her side with an update.

'I don't think Eli wants to play with us! Me and Keira's tried giving him egg and chips and he just don't take no notice of us! He won't even speak to us – he don't talk at all – he just sits there, sorta rocking.' She bends down and looks Eli in the eye again. 'Can you talk? P'raps he can't talk, we had some kids in our other class what never spoke hardly a single word.'

'Oh I think Eli can talk Amy. I think he's just a bit upset today and I'm sure he'll talk to us all as soon as he settles in, won't you Eli?' Ros addresses this last remark to Eli in the vain hope that she might at least get a nod of his head, but there is no response at all. Eli sits at the table, motionless, eyes cast down, just rocking slightly.

'Anyway, me and Keira's gunna play in the sand now. See you later Eli,' shouts Amy. As she grabs Keira's hand and makes for the sand, leaving Ros wondering how Keira or anyone else ever manages to get a word in edgeways!

Ros brings a beaker of milk, a couple of biscuits and some pieces of apple from the snack trolley and puts them on the table near Eli. He quickly picks the beaker up and drains it. While Eli eats his snack, Ros moves over to have a word with her TA, Lara.

'Have we got any information about Eli?' she says. 'He didn't come to the visits did he?'

'No,' says Lara, 'He didn't come to the visits so we haven't got an information form for him, and he didn't go to our Nursery class, or we'd know him. But I know his mum, she works in that little supermarket on the corner by the pub, and she's got quite a reputation locally. I go in there sometimes, but only when I run out of something.' Lara, like many TAs lives locally and is a good source of background information about the children and their families.

Insecurity and stress

Eli, like Sam in our third story, is feeling separation anxiety, an almost entirely male feeling. You would think that, by five and a half, Eli would be used to change, insecurity and stress. He is a child from a background where chaos and disruption are normal, and he has rarely known what is going to happen next. The only things he knows about school have come from mum and his grandma and we all know the urban myths about your first day at school!

No one has ever consulted Eli about what he would like, what to expect, how he might behave, so his anxiety, tears and constant searching of his mum's face are both natural and instinctive. Although she is certainly not very sympathetic to his feelings, she is the one person in this strange new world that he knows.

Schools usually offer pre-admission visits to children before they start, particularly if the child has not attended a pre-school setting. Eli is uncommon in that, despite the offer of a free nursery place, his mum didn't take it up, and hard-to-reach families such as Eli's are a great worry to teachers. They know that children who live in poverty, and specially those who don't come to the visits, are much slower to settle compared with children who do. They are also likely to make less progress during their first years at school, a gap that only gets wider as they get older. On the first day, familiarity is an important boost to children, and they are ready to get involved much sooner. However, Tracey never thought school was a place for her, she only attended sporadically herself, usually when the social worker pestered her mum, and she still avoids education most of the time, only appearing now, when she can take advantage of easy, free childminding and avoid a fine.

At this point, as he looks round this new world, Eli sees a place of order, colour and organisation, full of toys and games, all carefully maintained, with no pieces missing, no broken boxes, none of the muddle and mess he associates with playing at home when his mum is at work. These adults and the children are strangers to him. There are no familiar faces, and he doesn't even know where the toilet is!

So, as well as separation anxiety, Eli is suffering from stress, a feeling that is normal for him, but it is a different sort of stress from Sam's. Eli spends much of his time in stressful situations, where people are unpredictable, sometimes violent, and, as he gets older, using him as an easy target for blame or punishment. As described in Sam's story, stress in childhood comes in three sorts: the lowest level, sometimes referred to as *'positive stress'*, is the sort that all children experience when they visit the dentist, have a really disturbing nightmare, or have to cope with the death of a pet. This sort of stress is manageable and good for children, because it helps them to become resilient and trustful, knowing that their family will always be there for them.

The second sort of stress, called *'tolerable stress'*, which we wouldn't wish on any child, but happens to many: the divorce of their parents, the death of a relative, or even a disaster such as a tsunami or becoming a refugee. These are very significant experiences, but as long as the child has secure relationships with family members and those around them, they can survive without long-term damage.

However Eli is suffering from the third sort of stress, sometimes referred to as *'toxic stress'*, resulting from a chaotic home environment, extreme poverty, mental or physical abuse, or neglect. Toxic stress is present for Eli every day and during many nights, particularly those nights when his bedwetting and Tracey's drinking coincide. On these nights, he stays as still as he possibly can, hoping she won't come into the room and feel his bedclothes. If she does, he knows what will come next – a yank from bed into the cold air, onto the cold floor, followed by a poorly aimed, drunken slap. Eli's grandma usually intervenes at this stage, and strips him down, wrapping him roughly in a dry, but not usually clean blanket, and stripping the wet bedclothes off, saying, 'You'll be the death of me, all this washing,' as she grumbles off down the stairs again.

Impaired emotional development

This sort of continuous stress has actually hindered the growth of Eli's brain, making it both physically smaller and less responsive than those of other five year olds. The brains of babies who are neglected or abused are physically smaller than those of other babies, and Eli suffered neglect during Tracey's post-natal depression, when she gave him the physical care he needed to survive but not much more, and certainly not the loving attention most parents give their babies.

The best 'window in the brain' for emotional development is open for the first 18 months of a child's life, and if babies don't get the loving attention of their parents during this time, they may never learn how to relate properly to other people. Young babies of depressed mothers will obviously be more at risk in this aspect, as they often pick up messages from their mums, becoming withdrawn and sad themselves. Early stress will also have affected

Eli's immune system, probably causing his asthma and eczema, which are both linked to a defective immune system. Toxic stress has left Eli in a permanent state of high anxiety, which in some other children turns into unpredictable and aggressive behaviour, but in Eli results in stillness and silence – emotional shut-down.

Amy, who tries to befriend Eli, is lucky – even though she is also the child of a family in poverty, she has had a very different experience of family life, and as a girl, she is much more likely to have good language skills and to understand the feelings of others. Unlike Eli's mum and grandma, Amy's parents and sisters, her uncle and grandparents who live down the street, love her, are interested in her point of view, and show her how good speakers and listeners behave. They talked to Amy when she was a baby, played with her, sang to her, encouraged her to sing and to talk, and they have continued to nurture her as her brain and her language have improved.

Family situations

We have come a long way since the days when unmarried mothers were hidden away until their babies were born, only to lose those babies to adoption or to remain in the family as 'older sisters' to their own children. Life for the single mother is not so barren now, but many young parents today have lost the support of the old-fashioned family, where grandparents, parents, and children lived closely together, giving support, and often unconscious guidance to their children on parenting and the values of family relationships.

Many very young mothers are now cut loose from their families, living on estates full of other young families, where the only models of parenting are those gleaned from other inexperienced parents, or from magazine articles about celebrities or soap operas where the characters seem to dislike and put each other down, with frequent bad language and constant confrontation. Is it surprising that today's young parents follow these models, not just in the names they give their children, but in the way they bring them up?

Of course there are people who play the system, getting more in benefits than some of their neighbours earn in work, and this may seem unfair. But we cannot condemn the innocent children of parents like Tracey by driving them even further into poverty. Tracey is feckless, she didn't take advantage of the education system, the medical advice and contraception, the training she was offered, the courses she could have done through Surestart and later through Welfare to Work – but for Tracey the system is much too complicated, and full-time work would impose too much on her lifestyle! Like many people on benefit, the financial gains of full-time working would be small, and they would soon be swallowed up in bus fares or extra childcare.

Developmental difficulties

Even in the home corner, Eli is still trying to protect himself from rejection and further stress in the only way he knows – by withdrawing and refusing to get involved. When he does choose to talk, he will be difficult to understand, using a soft monotone as he speaks. The communication problem is made worse by his speech difficulties. Too-long use of a pacifier and bedtime bottle, poor nutrition and lazy speech in his family have resulted in the use of 'yike' and 'yook' instead of 'like' and 'look', 'nose' and 'vis' instead of 'those' and 'this'. Many children in poorer families also spend a lot of time watching TV and don't look at the real person in the room who is speaking to them – this results in lazy and immature speech, often left uncorrected by parents. Children who have a wide ranging diet (chewing helps speech muscles to develop), and plenty of conversations with adults and other children (a sense that what they say is interesting and valued) have better language, will have a head start at school, will get better jobs, and will be more successful throughout their lives than children with limited language like Eli.

When children feel stressed, their bodies go into the 'auto-pilot' of defence, which can take one of three forms: fight (hit out), flight (run away), or freeze (the behaviour of a rabbit caught in car headlights). Eli's favourite response to most situations is flight. He can run very fast and squeeze into very small spaces, and this is very useful when Tracey, and particularly Garry (her latest boyfriend) are trying to catch him. Under the bed, through the little gap in the back fence, behind the dustbins or the shed, even under piles of washing waiting for Tracey's attention; these are all places for a small and very quiet boy to hide until the trouble subsides, he is forgotten, or it gets dark and he can creep out again. However, when Eli knows flight is impossible or undesirable, he chooses to freeze, and he can stay passive and silent for long periods of time. In this state he is easy to lead around, he will stay wherever he is put, and he rarely causes any trouble as he just watches.

Let's return to Eli's first day:

Ros takes a basket of toy cars to the home corner, then decides to leave Eli for some time to play on his own. At least he seems to be a little more relaxed in the enclosed space of the home corner, and it leaves her free to talk to the other children who have started that morning. They are having no trouble settling in and are playing happily with all the new toys and equipment in the room. It is a pleasure to spend time with them, and when Ros looks at the clock she can hardly believe it is time to tidy up for group time and dinner. She decides to check on Eli, and visits the home corner again. For one moment she panics – Eli isn't on the chair, nor is he anywhere to be seen.

'Has anyone seen Eli?' she asks, trying to sound calm. Most of the children simply shake their heads, but Keira comes across and whispers in her ear.

''E's in the bed Miss.' She peels back the duvet on the home corner bed.

'Look Miss, he's gone fast asleep!' and sure enough, there is Eli, curled up at the bottom of the bed, dead to the world, with a toy car clutched in each hand.

'Thank you Keira,' Ros says, with genuine relief. 'We'll leave him to have a sleep while the rest of us have group time.'

Ros asks Lara to keep an eye on Eli as she leads the group session and organises the children for dinner. The noise of children washing their hands, or the smell from the dining hall wakes Eli, and with little persuasion from Lara, he joins them for dinner, greedily eating a jacket potato and cheese, mostly with his fingers. Lara talks quietly to the dining assistant, Chrissie, and asks her to keep a special eye on Eli in the playground, although no one thinks he will run away while there is a chance of more food.

When the children are safely in the dining hall, Ros and Lara sit down to talk about Eli. They are very concerned about him, and once they have got some information together they will talk to their headteacher and the coordinator for special needs. Eli is underweight and obviously late in developing social and emotional skills. However, the signs indicate neglect and poor parenting, not obvious violence, although they will both keep an eye on him for safeguarding issues, such as bruising. Some children have recently fallen through the net of support, and Nick, the head of the school, is very determined that no one in his school will suffer like those children whose parents have recently been in court and in the national news.

In many families like Tracey's, where no one has to get up in time to go to work, adults and children stay up late and get up late, meals are often casual and easy to eat with fingers or a spoon. Children are often late for school, or manage to get themselves there alone, both tired and hungry, the worst combination for learning. Eli is just the sort of child who gives immediate cause for concern, a 'vulnerable child', at risk in his life and in learning.

Ready for school

'School readiness' is a phrase recently adopted to describe the things children should know and be able to do in order to cope with school, become confident learners, understand the views of others, and develop into successful adults. Many children like Eli don't have these 'readiness for school' skills. They find it difficult to make friends, to use books and other resources, to understand what numbers and letters are for, and to express themselves appropriately. In England there has been a move to replace the current sensitive, whole child profile of learning, recorded over the last term of the early years (the Reception year) with a simpler 'school readiness' test in the first year of formal education. Such a test is similar to that administered in some other countries where children are already screened for school readiness at four, five or six.

A five-year-old child's vocabulary (not just the number of words they know, but the ability to use them) has been found to be the best predictor of whether they will or will not be able to escape poverty later in life. Ability to concentrate and pay attention are also 'school ready' skills, but Eli has difficulty with both of these because his body is always in a state of high stress and anxiety, flooded with hormones such as cortisol, which distract the parts of his brain that can help him to concentrate.

Other things that will affect Eli's 'school readiness' are that he has a poor diet, and, as we have seen, he doesn't have enough sleep. Families living in poverty are often forced to eat the cheapest foods, and these are not the most nutritious. Tracey often brings home 'past the sell-by date' food from work, but the ones she chooses often contain trans-fats and additives, and few of the ingredients that build strong bones, bodies and brains. On other days, cheap fast food, bread, chips and tinned beans make up the family diet, washed down with sugar-filled fizzy drinks.

What can be done to help Eli as he starts school?

When they find time to think of him, Eli is a bit of a puzzle to his family. They tolerate him, sometimes ignore him, and often shout at him, but no one ever thinks about trying to help him. Now he is at school, we can hope that his self-esteem will improve, and he will begin to make connections with other children. His teachers will do what they can to provide extra help as long as Eli comes to school regularly, and they can get Tracey to trust them. But first Eli will probably need to play out some of his past experiences using the toys, stories and other experiences offered in his classroom. This sort of therapeutic play will help him to manage starting school, but the long-term damage of his chaotic upbringing will remain with him throughout his life. Statistics show that children brought up in poverty are more likely to be unemployed, to spend time in prison, to be separated or divorced, and to suffer ill health, particularly if, like Eli, they were of low birth weight. He has drawn short straws in every important aspect:

- In **nature** – the genes Tracey handed down to him, with the damage done by poor diet, drink and drugs, and the heredity of poverty.
- In **nurture** – Tracey and her mum are not doing the best job here, for families like Tracey's, children are often seen as an accidental hazard, and parenting skills in this family are among the least helpful to Eli's future well-being.
- In **culture** – the culture of intense poverty is of missing, macho men and weak but willful women, aping soap opera relationships and wishing for celebrity status, which they will accept at any cost.
- In **chances** – the combination of chances which have left this child, not by his choice, in a state of poverty and the long-term implications of a life on the margins.

Of course, many families living in poverty, many lone parents, and some children living in stressful situations manage to live positive and fruitful lives, bringing up their children in the best way they can, to be good students and positive citizens, but they are the few. The love of good parents, positive early experiences, parents who would rather go without than see their children hungry, making the most of the little they have, keeping their homes warm, welcoming and comfortable are all gargantuan efforts when money is scarce, and telling these parents to go and get a job when there are none, to move house to find a job, when there are no houses they can afford, is an insult to these hard working families.

The haven or hell of school

Children who grow up without a bedroom or perhaps even a bed to call their own, no access to a computer or a quiet place to do their homework, second-hand uniforms and ill fitting shoes, no warm coat or gloves for the winter walk to school, and even leaving with no breakfast and no money for a school breakfast club are at a huge disadvantage. For these children, as with Eli, school can be a haven or a hell, a haven of respite, warmth, kindness and even food, or a hell of teasing, bullying, missed targets, lost PE kit, or unfair blame for a life that is out of control.

We all hope that school will turn out to be the haven of peace and organisation that Eli needs, but it will be hard work for him and for his teacher, as he is so far behind most of the other children in the class, and we already know that he won't get much help from home. He finds it difficult to speak out and to make friends, so joining in and contributing to class activities will be hard work for everyone. Amy's early experiences of family meals, simple walks and outings, being with her parents and older sisters all helped her to develop readiness for school. She will be well ahead of Eli in early reading and number skills, experience of books, using scissors, cutlery and other tools such as pencils. Although Eli has spent much of his time out of doors and is able to climb, run, swing and ride a bike, he has not had much chance to learn about books, drawing, or use fine motor skills, which lead to reading, writing and maths. His version of sitting still and listening only catapults him back into stress as he remembers the times when he needs to do this at home. So even his ability to sit very still turns into a disadvantage.

Secure environment

Eli needs stability and security. He needs time to get to know his teacher and to make friends. He feels abandoned and depressed, so he needs to feel wanted and valued for what he can do and what he can offer. Plenty of time to play alone and with other children will help, but he is not used to having the sorts of toys and games that are in his classroom. The garden outside the classroom is even more different from home. At home, the broken toys, bikes, bags of discarded rubbish and furniture clutter the garden, and have become Eli's playground and den. Occasionally the local boys see Eli peeping over the back fence and invite him to join a football game in the park, but more often, he is just left to watch and wander at the edge of the pitch. The garden at school is very different, full of well maintained outdoor toys and equipment, but with rules about sharing, care and organisation that are hard for Eli to understand. His poor language means that when he can summon up the courage to get involved, he grabs, throws, and tosses things aside. Because he has no toys at home, he hides favourite things in pockets and corners, and he knows absolutely nothing about clearing up, all of which infuriate the other children. Fortunately, his teacher understands his problems and she will work hard to hep Eli to find a place and a voice in her class, to become included in children's games and activities. If he can't or won't talk to other children, and learn to become a member of the class, they will soon abandon him and he will become an outsider in school, as he has become an outsider at home.

If all the children in Ros's class were as school ready as Amy, Ros's job would be much easier. While she is struggling with so many children like Eli, with such intense needs, she is spreading herself too thinly to be really effective. Early intervention, through parenting classes, advice to young, pregnant women and their partners, and concentrating on the period from birth to three, could remove this problem from our schools, leaving teachers and children to concentrate on learning through play and talk in the first years, and giving them a really good educational start. In Scandinavian countries, teachers wait until children are seven or even eight before starting formal learning, spending the first years of school making sure children have the social and physical skills in place. Following this system, Scandinavian countries continue to lead Europe in academic achievement at 11, including the teaching of a second language (English) to all children. In England we start too soon, go too fast and consequently fail at 11, slipping below mid-way in the international comparison tables.

Positive support

In planning for Eli, Ros will begin by considering all the options she has for helping Eli. She could try:

- **Speech therapy** to help with the production of language. The difficulties with this service are not only the shortage of therapists, which is a national problem, but the clinic is at the Health Centre, and parents must take responsibility for the treatment. Tracey has been pretty resistant to outside support in the past, and would probably lose Eli's entitlement by missing appointments, and not practising the exercises at home.

- **Referral to a speech and language therapist** or specialist teacher for help with his communication skills. There are far more children who need these services than the heath authorities can provide, so Eli may well be much older before he comes to the top of the list, and by that time the problems may be difficult to cure. The school will also need Tracey's permission, and a commitment from her to follow the advice of the therapist.

- **The nurture group in school**, where talking, music, rhythm and drama are used to help with physical skills and motor control. Working in a small group might also help Eli's confidence in using language. Nurture groups are often staffed by the release of a member of the school staff who has been trained in the appropriate techniques. One of the TAs leads the group at Eli's school, working with small groups for short periods during the school day.

- **Involvement of the school nurse**. This school is fortunate in that, because of the large number of deprived families in the catchment area, they do have visits from a school nurse, who is prepared to make home visits to families and involve other agencies to help where necessary. Of course, Tracey may not welcome this sort of contact.

Ros will also take note of the curriculum guidance that children who have not yet reached readiness for school and the curriculum for Year 1, '*should continue to follow the curriculum for the Early Years Foundation Stage to develop their word reading, spelling and language skills.*' (DFE 2013) This will allow her to adapt her planning to take into account the needs of Eli and any other children whose language development is delayed, but it will increase the planning load for her as she co-ordinates two developmental groups.

There are currently huge pressures on teachers in Year 1 classes to get on with formal learning, reading, writing and calculating, even when it is obvious that the children are not yet ready. These pressures mean that children are faced with a sudden and inappropriate change from a sensitive balance of adult-initiated and child-initiated activity, to a programme dominated by adult planned tasks and whole group teaching. Fortunately, in Ros's school the teachers in Year 1 are encouraged to follow an early years curriculum for at least the first term, giving the less mature children links with their previous experiences as they make the transfer to more formal learning. If she thinks Eli needs it, Ros will also borrow some equipment and resources from the nursery class, and make this available to Eli and other children who are finding transition difficult.

We already know that children who are born in the summer months often find it harder to transfer to a more adult directed programme, because their bodies still need movement, outdoor experiences, sensory materials and plenty of time to play and talk. There are other groups of children who are also at risk of a real dip in their learning and motivation at transition. These include:

- Children who speak **English as an additional language**, and are working hard to maintain both.
- Children who have **learning difficulties or disabilities**, including delayed development or communication.
- Children who qualify for **free school meals** or other subsidies from government such as any Pupil Premium.
- Many **boys**, who generally develop the skills of sitting and listening, and fine motor ability later than many girls.

Of course, some children appear in several of these categories, making it even more likely that they will struggle. Continuity for children as they move from one stage of education to another is vital, and that sense of continuity must be underpinned by a calm continuation of the familiar, with an injection of progression to the next stage.

Schools that achieve this magical continuity in learning follow the same sorts of models. Some of the features of these models are:

- View moving on as a process not an event.
  - Support active, independent learning; limit time spent sitting and listening.
  - Ensure play-based activities, routines and resources continue beyond the early years.
  - Include more than one strategy for supporting transition.
  - Consider individual needs, particularly those of younger/less mature children, those who are less able, have additional learning needs or English as an additional language, and boys.
  - Ensure that children's friendships are maintained.
  - Include some release time for practitioners to visit each other's classes, see how the children learn, and discuss them with their current teachers.
  - Where possible, enable staff to move and 'move up' with the children.

These strategies should ensure that children like Eli get the support they need as they move into the next stage of their learning.

An effective learning environment for children just moving into statutory schooling

One of the problems for Ros and her colleagues is that Eli still needs an environment where he can feel safe, can choose his own path through learning, and can play out the features of his home life that are preventing him from engaging with learning. He will never learn to talk, to read, to write stories or to make friends without the sort of experience that more fortunate under-fives have had. His delayed development, which is partly due to poor nutrition, but more importantly to lack of stimulation and loving care, will take time to put right, and maybe he will never catch up. He is not the only one in the year group, there are children like him in each group in Ros's school. If their needs are not catered for, some of them can cause a real problem as they wrestle with the need to sit still and listen, filling their small bodies with cortisol and testosterone, and eventually exploding in unacceptable behaviours such as temper tantrums, defiance and even violence to other children.

However, Ros has a duty to Amy, Keira and other children who have had different experiences and are developing rapidly into fluent speakers, attentive listeners and sociable friends. These children need challenge to spark their interest, purposeful extensions to their play, which don't cramp their imaginations and give them plenty of opportunities to develop their skills. How to release the potential of these children, while still catering for the needs of Eli, will stretch Ros's professionalism and teaching skills to the limits. She will work hard to plan well-matched tasks for all the children in her class, but she knows that children like Eli are less likely to succeed in school, or in later life. For them, the mix of nature, nurture, culture and chance, much of it decided at conception, is often just too high a mountain to climb, even with the support of the very best teachers. He is lucky that his first taste of what his gran calls 'big school' is with Ros and her colleagues, who are making real efforts to make transition into school a seamless process. There are many other children like Eli who are less fortunate, and may be doomed to inappropriate and insensitive experiences at school and poverty at home, combining to make them feel a failure in both places.

A message from Eli

School is like a film on TV for me. I've never seen so many toys, but I don't like being watched all the time, it makes me scared and excited all at once. There's so much to do, and it's hard to choose, so sometimes I don't do anything, and other times I put things in my pocket so other kids won't get them first. I really like the little people in the brick box, and the Batman cloak in the dressing-up box. Sometimes I wear it to give me superpowers so I won't cry. Everyone would like me if I really did have superpowers. I'd get my mum and my gran a new house, and some new clothes, and a load of toys for the baby. I'd get loads of chocolate for me, but I wouldn't get anything for my new uncle Len, he pretends to like me, but he hits me sometimes when my mum isn't looking.

Practitioners

- How do you reach the 'unreachable' parents like Tracey, whose children are invisible to the education system until they arrive on the first day of term?
- Eli hasn't had the advantage of a pre-school education. How would you begin to meet his needs without damaging the provision for the other children in the class?
- Is there a place for 'keeping back' children who are not ready for the programme in the year group for their chronological age? There is a nursery class at Eli's school. Would you support moving him into the nursery for a term so he can begin to catch up?
- If you could list the skills and abilities a child needs to be ready for school, what would be on your list? What does a school need to do to be ready for Eli?

Parents

- Remember, your child only starts school once, and you really need to get it right! Pre-entry visits and other preparation activities are very important for all children. Most children can't remember their first day at nursery, daycare or child-minder's, so it is another 'home' for them, and leaving the safety of daycare to go to school is a very big step, even for the most confident child.
- If your child is an only child, or the oldest of your children this is a first for you too. What are the most important things for you to know about the school, so you can prepare your child for this move?
- What are the most important things about your child that you need to tell the teachers?

Interlude 5 Hands on, brains on: movement and learning

'For most students academic learning is too abstract. They need to see, touch and smell what they read and write about.'

John Goodland educational researcher and theorist

'Tell me and I forget, teach me and I may remember, involve me and I learn.'

Benjamin Franklin

All children need to move as they learn, as both the moving and the tactile experiences reinforce the stimuli entering the brain. Movements that appear to activate the brain and support learning, and those that most children love, include spinning, swinging, rocking, and hanging upside down. These skills, which make learning out of doors so exciting and rewarding, are no longer in demand in primary classrooms, many of which do not even have access to learning outdoors. Those large muscles in legs, arms, shoulders and thighs are suddenly a handicap as boys are expected to sit for long periods, controlling their limbs and even sitting cross-legged on the floor, where they are in danger of just rolling over. One boy at this stage summed up his feelings when he said to a researcher 'Carpet, carpet, carpet, work, work, work. Wastes your time, wastes your life.'

However, movements helps to develop the cerebellum, which has vital connections with balance and memory. From the gentle motion of the pregnant mother as she sways to the music on the radio, the father rocking his baby to sleep, to the toddler on the rocking horse or the nursery children on their climbing frames and bikes, repetitive movement is a key element in learning, transferring short-term memory to long-term storage. It is a shame that in some places swings, roundabouts, rocking seats and slides have been removed or are 'off limits' to many children in an attempt to keep them safe. Knowing that these repetitive movements help children's learning should remind us of the importance of such activities and prompt us to provide as many opportunities as we can for children to engage in them. If you have a tree in your setting or your garden, get a rope and a tyre – you won't regret it!

The importance of whole-body play

The nervous system provides the tools for young scientists and explorers, and physical, whole-body play is often referred to as sensory motor exploration, combining the senses and movement. In settings for babies and toddlers, the practitioners realise that the children they work with will want to spend most of their time just exploring the things around them, with their whole bodies. A baby will become absorbed in looking at a waving leaf, tracing a pattern in juice spilt on the table, or stroking a piece of furry fabric. An older child can be distracted by an ant on their skin, a hole in the pavement, a turning doorknob, water flowing from a tap, or a lorry unloading sand outside the nursery fence. These sensory stimuli will be much more powerful than the last thing the child was doing, or the activity the adult has planned. Distractibility is a normal feature of nursery life, and is usually treated with respect and tolerance. The generally flexible and unhurried pace of the session allows for such distractions, even building on them as stimuli for further learning and language.

Most scientists agree that play is a vital way to learn, and all young animals play, but some need more play than others, and humans are among these. The reason why humans have such a long childhood is that we need more time to play, because it is through play that we build our bigger brains. Research into the behaviour of primates has helped, as the size and power of the brains of different species directly reflects the amount of play they are involved in. Higher order apes, such as chimpanzees, gorillas and orang-utans, spend much more of their younger years playing, and don't reach adulthood until much later than other apes.

In humans, movement stimulates the cerebellum and the neo-cortex, and this appears to affect the level of synaptogenesis (the production of links between brain cells), giving the active body a more powerful brain.

Self-activated learning

Eli's early life has been filled with self-activated learning, using junk he finds around the house and outside, so he has made links in his brain through movement, but the level of stress hormones in his body and brain constantly erodes these links, inhibiting any myelination, and reducing his brain to a collection of random impulses. The only myelinated links are those related to knowing when to keep quiet, and the good places to hide from trouble. Eli will also have learned how to get the most from his mum and grandma, reading expressions and body language, and sensing the times when he is likely to get treats or the occasional rough cuddle. One important quality for humans is the ability to read others' expressions and body language, and this needs activity in both sides of the brain and is usually a female attribute. In Eli's case, the need for survival has shaped his brain into more female structures.

He is not used to having many toys, and those he does get are of poor quality and limited learning value. Like most poor children, he will make a toy from anything, and he uses the junk in the garden to make his own toys which reflect the TV and DVD he watches. Sticks become guns and his coat becomes a superhero cloak. Books are uncommon and what his gran calls her 'books' are women's magazines and shopping catalogues, which Eli is not allowed to touch.

What he desperately needs is adult support and help to structure his play and involve others in it. He will need help in knowing how to play with the resources in school, as he is not used to any sort of order or organisation. He will also need help in restraining his own movements to play with smaller, more intricate equipment. He still uses a 'palmar' grip, holding pens, tools and equipment in his fist, resulting in a heavy, imprecise action when drawing or painting. A 'pincer' grip is hard for some children to learn, and the stresses involved in mark making and writing may result in pain and even a sort of spasm as these children struggle to write.

In movement and in play we activate the nervous system, and lay down pathways for later learning. Some of these pathways are physical commands to parts of our body – how to cushion the jump from a climbing frame, how to ride a bike, how to pour without spilling, and these skills are some of Eli's strengths. He has agility and stamina and is surprisingly agile and strong for such a timid, skinny little boy.

Other pathways built through action in play are much more subtle, supporting our relationships, or controlling our behaviour when we are with others. These involve us in watching movements of bodies and expressions on faces as we interact with others, and are practised in 'counterfactual' or pretend play. His experience with his family has made him good at reading body language, but not always at responding.

Role-play

Danni, however, has had a different life, with different experiences of home and family. When she is involved in role-play, she is practising her social and creative skills too, and replaying the situations she sees at home and in the media will build up resilience to stresses later in real life by giving her practice in trying on different ways of responding. At this age, girls often become excellent mimics of adults and other children, copying voices, expressions and gestures with uncanny accuracy. A child playing her own mother in the home corner, or a bossy shopkeeper in the outdoor shop will give plenty of clues to the ways she has observed and can imitate others she meets. Boys will tend to make more direct connections with sports people, superheroes and other male role models, perhaps because they have less opportunity to see their fathers doing as wide a range of activities as their mothers. Counterfactual play for boys is much more active, with big movements of the limbs and body, preferably out of doors and with a range of weapons (often home-made) to conquer the baddies and rescue the innocent. Sadly, it is rare to see boys copying the gentler side of relationships through role-play, and those who do may risk teasing or sideways glances from other children and even the adults around them.

Counterfactual play

Through active play, Eli and Danni and all their friends are learning to be young problem-solvers and thinkers in their counterfactual lives, getting practice in approaching the challenges they see other people dealing with. Children with plenty of counterfactual play practice seem to become better problem solvers later, and although Eli's counterfactual activities have been very limited, he already has the potential to use his experiences as a basis for future learning.

If you take a time-lapse film of children sitting listening to a story, you will see a movement that looks like seaweed, wafting to and fro under the sea, always moving, never still. Young children still don't have the ability to keep their bodies completely still, and when they are learning anything, they need to move. Think of the child who fiddles with the end of her ponytail as she moves small world figures with her other hand; the boy who repeatedly undoes and does up the Velcro on his trainers while he listens to a story; the swayers, the jigglers, the rockers and the thumb suckers; somehow, these movements help the child to concentrate and even to keep the rest of their body still.

You may also see 'echoing' of limbs as young children paint or draw, with the non-dominant hand following the dominant one. Some children also echo movements they see when others are eating or talking, moving their own limbs to echo movements on the other side of their bodies. Others hold one hand with the other, lean on their hand to hold their head still, or squint, putting their hands round their eyes to help with focus. These are all early control practice, and sometimes the child has not had enough practice to control two hands, feet or arms doing different actions, so they 'echo' each other. Because the left side of the brain controls the right side of the body, and vice versa, the messages sometime get confused, particularly if the movement requires links between the two.

Again, young boys may find it more difficult than girls to manage both sides of their body in coordinated movements, because the links through the corpus callosum between the hemispheres are not yet strong enough. Boys are naturally good at activities involving spatial awareness and their movement skills are often developed before those of girls, but orchestrating both sides of the brain to make the movements smoothly coordinated is more difficult for boys, and a dominant hand may emerge later in some boys. Both boys and girls need practice in using both hands together before perfecting the use of one or the other, so resources such as construction sets, malleable materials such as play dough, playing musical instruments, and plenty of outdoor play will help them all.

The muscles needed for writing are not just located in children's dominant hands, they are in their wrists, arms, shoulders, backs and even their legs and feet, as they keep their whole body in balance – steadying the paper and keeping control of the pencil. It is no wonder that some children, and young boys in particular, find this concentration so tiring and unpleasant that they avoid it or spend the least possible time doing it. Children who are just learning to read and write, will often rest their head on their arm or hand – we may think they are tired, but many of them are keeping their heads still and the right distance from the page for optimum focal length. Other children like to lie down to concentrate, to sit with their feet folded under them, or to wind their legs round the chair. Keeping still is hard, and takes lots of practice, and meanwhile, children will invent their own ways of restraining the bits of their bodies they don't need at the moment. Doing this and writing something acceptable must seem an impossible task for some children.

Boys and girls at play

Boys and girls differ in the amount of full body, active play they choose to engage in. Most boys love to run, ride, climb, dig, pour, balance, swing, and seem to need to move to learn anything. If they don't get enough active play during the day, they store up stress, which makes them fidgety, noisy and aggressive when we need them to concentrate. These chemicals also seem to make them less able to listen or hear what is said to them, and less able to sustain interest, even in things that would otherwise appeal to them. Experienced practitioners and teachers recognise this frustration, which often occurs when the weather is bad, or when children have not had enough time for full body play, and they compensate by offering children a chance to run around or do some vigorous, whole-body movement, before sessions when they must sit and listen. A short burst of activity will dissipate the frustration building up in children's bodies and enable them to manage their bodies in the more concentrated time that follows.

To get some sense of order in their group times, practitioners and teachers would be well advised to follow Danni's teacher and offer early warnings and a time for letting off steam before embarking on an adult-led activity. This has two purposes – to let the boys run off excess energy, but also to get the girls up to speed.

In their early years, many boys' games involve bodily contact, tumbling, and continuous flow of action, and they are far more interested in objects and things (props, capes, guns, swords, etc.) than in people, feelings or the consequences of their actions. Because they often have a shorter attention span they will flow from activity to activity seemingly without communicating with each other, almost like a flock of birds.

Eli is very agile and physically quite fit, although thin and very small for his age. Most of the exercise he has taken has been self-generated, in the garden and inside at home. He will find it difficult to join groups of boys as they play at school, partly because of his language limitations and partly because he has never had to negotiate, follow rules, or plan his play with anyone else.

There is no chance that Eli will overeat and become obese, but his diet of fast food and the 'past the sell-by date' food Tracey brings home fails to provide him with the high quality nutrition of more fortunate children. He is used to the short 'highs' of sugar and fat rich foods, and his body has not had the satisfaction of the 'slow-burn' of whole grains, lean meats, vegetables and fruits. As he gets older, Eli risks becoming a fast food and cheap beer 'couch potato' with all the risks that entails.

Many girls of Eli's age choose to play in a quieter way than boys, often sitting and chatting with their friends, involved in quiet collaborative or imaginative games, moving about more slowly, often staying near adults. Whether this behaviour is affected by nature, nurture or culture, it often means that girls get plenty of experience of watching adults but insufficient active play to get into healthy habits, or develop their physical skills. By adolescence many girls face problems with their weight and general physical fitness. They should be encouraged to spend time out of doors and in lively physical exercise, either with other girls, in games with boys, or in adult-led, whole-group physical activities. These should include games using balls, hoops, and other equipment to improve girls' catching and throwing skills, and running and jumping to improve strength and stamina. Playing ring games and simple team games will appeal to their sense of collaboration, while the boys will enjoy the competition.

For many years, educationalists discouraged the use of fingers for counting, but now we realise that a child with a kinaesthetic learning style will certainly benefit from the sensation of using his fingers as he counts, and not feel guilty for using these portable, ever available calculation tools. Most children need 'manipulatives' or concrete resources for learning, whether these are wooden blocks, plastic coins, or toy cars, small world figures or sand, water and play dough. Surprisingly, girls appear to find the use of manipulatives helps them with maths, and these should be offered to all children right through the primary years.

Not all children will become Olympic athletes, but with adult encouragement they can use their bodies as powerful learning tools to improve their brains. Inside and outside our classrooms and settings, children have a right to physical activity and we can't leave this to playtimes, occasional PE lessons, and possible physical activity after school. We must build on the experiences children have in nursery and Reception classes, and use the outdoor environment for learning, in independent and more formal adult-led sessions. We must resist the pressure for more recorded work, the over emphasis on reading and writing. Bad weather, small spaces, inaccessible equipment, or children in less than appropriate clothing or footwear, to say nothing of the problems of getting undressed and finding the right clothes at the end of a session can all be used as excuses. These difficulties can all be overcome by an adult who knows the importance of movement play for young children, and is determined to ensure the right of every child to move as they learn.

Add some musical movement

At every stage, music is helpful in enhancing children's learning and their memories. There are many theories about why listening and responding to music improve learning, and some are:

- The part of the brain that processes movement (the motor cortex) is very near the one processing memory (the cerebellum). Play and practical activities make learning easier, so moving to music will help children to retain what they are learning. Music can help us to remember things, particularly if the music is the same when we are remembering and recalling. An example of this would be the triggers in advertising music. Most adults can remember the jingles for 'Hands that do dishes', 'Nuts, whole hazel nuts', 'Just one Cornetto', or more recently 'Go compare!'. These 'sticky' tunes get into our brains and we only have to hear the first note and we are off! Wise and imaginative practitioners and teachers use the power of simple jingles, nursery rhymes and memorable tunes to help children to remember spellings, number facts and other important pieces of information. One school stopped sending notes home to parents and taught the children a simple 'message song' to be used when information needed to be communicated to parents. They also recorded the song for the website, to remind parents of the messages. It's amazing how much more powerful a simple tune can be than a piece of paper lost in the washing machine!

- The inner ear plays an important part in our physical balance. It affects our sight and focus, our ability to hear with both ears and move with confidence and control. Rocking and swinging can contribute to the way we stabilise images on our retinas, enabling us to recognise such things as the differences between letter and word shapes. Stimulation of the inner ear in this way also helps physical balance and motor coordination, both vital to future success in learning. Gentle rocking and swaying movements will help to fix information and deepen learning. Music is one of the best ways to stimulate these movements.

- Phonological awareness, the ability to hear and discriminate between sounds is an essential tool in learning to read. Listening to music is now proven to improve phonological awareness. Children who listen to music regularly (they don't have to be playing an instrument) become better readers, who are more likely to be able to use phonics. Including music in some parts of the day will have a positive effect on learning and on general mood in the room – but don't make it into 'wallpaper' by playing music all the time, and don't have the music too loud, or it will impair the learning environment for some children.

- If music is accompanied by movement – even clapping, foot tapping or head nodding in time to the music – it will trigger neurons which will have a sort of ripple effect in the cells near the cerebellum, which process the movement. These ripples will improve attention and memory, and in future, we may find this has an effect on the electrical impulses right across the brain – that brain waves really do respond to music. Maybe we should stop saying 'Take your headphones off!' to our teenagers when they are doing their homework, as long as they really are listening to music.

- A daily physical movement session for children of all ages, with or without music, promotes academic performance and improves the attitude to learning. Exercise should be moderately vigorous, and last for around 30 minutes, raising the heart rate and making them (and us) out of breath. Outdoor play at a leisurely pace is not enough, children should experience physical activity in adult-led sessions both indoors and outside. If this vigorous movement is accompanied by singing or music, it will be even more effective.

- Take a break. Even as adults, we find that when we have been concentrating hard, a singing session, a walk, a swim or a visit to the gym, revives us and reduces stress. We all feel better when we have done it, returning to our work with more energy and concentration. Children need breaks too, and we sometimes ask them to move from one sedentary task to another without a break to relax and re-energise. Using ribbon sticks to move and dance on the way back from assembly will result in better attention when you need to explain what will happen next; a quick run round the playground before or after a 'big write' will help to let of steam. This sort of movement break appears to help some boys, and particularly the type of boy who is never still, even when they are concentrating. They are the jigglers and fiddlers who can learn better if they are on the move, and these boys may also become the adult men who still jiggle while chatting at the bar, or tap their feet as they enjoy a meal. Two more successful strategies have been to start the day with a movement session in every class, or to offer fidgety children stress balls or small soft toys to handle during whole group sessions where they are expected to do lots of listening.

- Clapping, tapping and moving in a steady beat, particularly when both hands are involved, really appears to help young children to concentrate and remember things. Clapping along to nursery rhymes and songs, phonic rhymes and rhyming stories all reinforce what children are singing or saying. The rhymes do not need tunes, just tap or clap to the rhythm. Small blocks of wood, rhythm sticks, or even chopsticks in each hand provide an incentive to keep in time.

- Cross it over – as we have seen earlier in this interlude, the left side of the brain has a controlling influence on the right side of the body and the right hemisphere controls the left. Activities that involve both brain hemispheres, and both hands, feet, eyes, ears are very powerful learning tools. In some early years settings, practitioners have made reminder lists of the sorts of activities that activate both sides of the brain, and most of these are very familiar: riding wheeled toys, climbing, playing simple instruments, woodwork, pouring, cutting, drawing, painting, construction toys. These are all important, and those which use the child's whole body will be powerful learning activities, forging links across the corpus callosum between the two sides of the brain. Playing with play dough and clay, 'gloop' and 'slime', cooking, sand, water and mud, all help to strengthen muscles in fingers and hands, and prepare the body and brain for the complex tasks of reading and writing. Making marks with two brushes, chalks or felt pens, or using both hands in cornflour or finger paint are others, in fact nothing in a good early years room should be described as 'just play'; it's brain building in action.

Activities where the hands move past the mid-line in the body into the space on the other side are particularly powerful in stretching the brain's boundaries. We could use adult-imposed exercises to offer this, and some schools and settings do use Brain Gym, but simple, everyday activities can offer complex movements: putting on your coat by yourself, turning the pages in a picture book or magazine, sharing out the cards for a word game, tying shoelaces or the ties on an apron, returning bricks to the box, or even singing 'Heads, shoulders, knees and toes' with your arms crossed can be incorporated into the day.

Add some music and you will add more power to the movement. Movement and music are at the heart of good early years practice. Even though many of us may be planning

activities because the guidance tells us to, because experience has shown that it works, or because we feel in our hearts that is what children like to do, we now have indisputable evidence that children need to move, to sing, to clap, to dance, not just for enjoyment, but because that is the way they switch on their brains and make learning permanent. The pressure cooker of some practice, where children are sitting down and required to sit still for large portions of the day, will have a lasting effect on their learning and we will risk losing the joy and wonder of exploring the world, that should be in the eyes of every young child, and especially those blue eyes of children like Eli.

A word about the senses

Activities that trigger the five senses of sight, hearing, touch, smell, and taste are among the most powerful learning tools. Think of the perfume your mother uses, the sight of a sunny beach, the sound of a blackbird in the twilight, the flavour of those sweets you loved as a child and can't get any more. These triggers are all sensory memories. Remember that a daily physical exercise session will activate the brain and promote sight, touch and hearing.

Experienced early years teachers and practitioners are used to providing for the five senses, through matching games and spot the difference; sound boxes and listening games; feely bags and silky dough; smelling bottles and herbal pillows; cooking and experiencing food. These are all familiar ways to engage children in learning through their senses.

However, if we can include two or more senses in one experience, it doubles the power and triggers deeper learning. It also provides 'learning hooks' for children with different learning styles and preferences. The child who is mainly a visual learner will respond well to looking at pictures and objects, but the predominantly kinaesthetic learner will be more engaged if she can hold the object too. Sounds may well help the child who is primarily an auditory learner to learn as they listen.

Here are some examples of teachers who try to stimulate children's senses as they work:

- When telling stories, Claire always asks the children to think of what the places smell like as well as what they look like. She also asks them to make the sounds of the story, either with their voices or using simple instruments. At some points in the story she will ask the children to imagine what they would see if they turned round, or looked at the ground. In this way, the children really feel they are experiencing the story with all their senses.

- Marie has a 'five senses' technique she uses when she goes out on a walk or visit with her class. She knows that different children will notice and remember different things, some of which she won't even have noticed herself. So when they get back from the visit, she asks the children what they have seen, what they heard, what they touched, smelled or tasted. They mind map all this information, helping the children to remember everything they experienced.

- Ros and her TA, Lara, have a gentle competition to see how many senses they can trigger through the range of play materials they offer. This might be black dough perfumed with coffee and some coffee beans mixed in; some old saucepans tied to the fence with chopstick beaters; pink and purple perfumed puffy paint; making bread and baking it in school so everyone can smell and taste it; walking barefoot on painty, popping bubble wrap; or a gentle game of blindfold to encourage the use of the other senses.

- Greg tries to use colour to stimulate learning in his room. He has collected a range of drapes and coloured objects, and uses these to quickly change the mood in his talking corner or creative area. He uses red and yellow in his creative and role-play areas when he wants the children to be lively and imaginative, blue and green for calming and peacefulness, and neutral colours like brown and beige to promote positive feelings and security. He also knows that red, dark blue, dark green and black are all action colours, chosen by superheroes, so he uses these to enhance spaces out of doors where superheroes can play, stimulated by the colours of their heroes.

- Mina tries to make the nursery setting home-like for the very young children there. She provides textures such as soft wool, fleece and cushions, pictures and ornaments to make the room look more like home, she sometimes plays the radio very softly in the background, or uses a CD of water flowing, or the sea, and she often cooks simple foods to provide sensory input for the babies and toddlers who may be missing these stimuli at home.

- In Ola's garden outside her classroom, she has helped the children to plant herbs and perfumed flowers, shrubs with textured foliage, some tomato plants in a grow-bag, and a willow den where the children can sit to read or just be. Shells and old CDs hang from the big tree by the fence, and some little bells jingle in the breeze. The children fill bird feeders and watch the birds come to feed. Ola has put a little speaker under a bench where it can play a bird song CD, and there is a digging area where children can experience the fun of just digging.

Movement control

When they are very young, babies move all the time because they haven't yet achieved control of their muscles. They move all their limbs at once, and when they look at their waving feet or hands, to start with they don't even realise they belong to them.

As children grow older, however, this distractibility can get in the way of the planned 'programme' and children who can't manage distractions when they need to, will be disadvantaged, particularly when they are in a group activity led by a teacher. What can be an advantage for a young scientist when exploring new activities in a self-initiated game can be a major problem for both child and teacher at group or whole class times. In these cases practitioners find it useful if they:

- Give a 'two minute warning' before a change of task, particularly from child-initiated sessions to more formal, adult-led times.

- Use a clapping pattern, a hand signal or a 'clearing up song' to help children keep up the momentum of clearing up and changing activity.

- Encourage children who are easily distracted to sit near the front of the group, or with an additional member of staff, where a touch of the hand can help maintain concentration.

- Plan for short periods of physical movement, such as action songs, movement rhymes or 'Simon says', before expecting children to sit still and listen, and during the session.

- Use the child's name regularly to regain eye contact and attention.

- Practise the physical features and skills of listening, such as looking at the speaker and 'good sitting'. When asked to define 'good sitting' one group of five year olds came up with this description: 'Put your bottom on the carpet. Cross your legs. Put your hands on your knees. Sit up straight. Look at Mrs Parker. Switch on your listening.' And finally – 'Make your face like this,' said one girl opening her eyes wide, and giving a big smile with her lips firmly closed – Mrs Parker would be proud of her.

- Finally, make sure you don't go on too long! It is accepted now that a four-year-old child can concentrate and stay still for twice the number of minutes as their age in years, plus or minus a minute. That's between seven and nine minutes for a group of four year olds before they lose concentration, although the most well-behaved will probably be able to hide it. Of course, you don't need to reduce your planned sessions for these four year olds to eight minutes each, you just need to make sure that every eight minutes or so, you insert some change – a song, a rhyme, a movement activity, a contribution from a child, a chance to chat to a talk partner, use a finger puppet, or even just 'stand up, turn round, sit down again'.

There is no doubt that children need to move, and that movement will enhance learning, it's just important to get the movement and the attention balance right – and remember that too much sitting and listening can produce stress chemicals that block learning.

Never forget the importance of involving the whole body and all the senses in learning activities. Eli and all the children in his class continue to need a wide range of stimuli for their bodies and their senses as they move from the early years into school, and Eli in particular, may need help to recognise his sensory experiences through a language support programme.

Eventually, with the right sorts of experience, most children achieve the levels of gross motor skill to move and manage their bodies, fine motor skills to handle pencils and other tools, and visual skills needed to differentiate between individual letter and number shapes for reading writing and maths. What is amazing about the human brain is that most children do achieve these levels of skill, somewhere between the ages of four and eight – the range of normal development.

Points to ponder

- Movement is vital for all children yet much of our educational intention is to encourage sitting still and listening. How can settings and schools ensure that children get enough movement experience before they embark on activities where concentration is vital?

- Eli, and children like him, are used to moving all the time and find sitting still almost impossible. What would be some good ways to help him to feel more secure?

- Distractibility is a feature of all young children, who become entranced by small things and events, losing concentration on what you want. In this interlude, there are some ideas from practitioners and teachers. Which of these do you use? Are there any ideas you could adopt?

- How can you help children who are very agile and physically skilled in gross motor activities, but very poor at fine motor control? How could practitioners involve their parents?

- Do you use music in your classroom or nursery? Share thoughts and ideas about using music to improve concentration and learning.

- Eli loves wearing the superhero cloak. How could you help children like Eli who have not had much experience of group play, to integrate and negotiate with other children?

- How could settings and schools help parents to improve the diet of their children and families to ensure they are ready to learn?

Stage 6 Missing you, but moving on – Ruby is six

'Learning, in my view, is more than acquiring information. It's a social activity that leads to more complex ways of thinking, which is as much a function of the space between us as it is a product of what happens in our own heads. When the space between people contains trust, engagement and positive regard, the capacity for cognitive, emotional, and physiological changes is greater. Professional development leaders can increase learning by actively cultivating richer, more positive connections among people. That would have a higher yield of professional learning than the importation of experts who dispense lots of information.'

Jane E. Dutton, writer

If you follow a six or seven year old child taking a message to a class in the nursery, you may see something like this:

Beth, carefully carrying boxes of felt pens and some whiteboards opens the door of the nursery and steps inside. She walks through the activities going on there, past children on the floor with big bricks, round a girl carrying the nursery guinea pig towards the book corner for a story, and under waving fronds of 'seaweed' hanging from the ceiling to make an underwater cave. She can't immediately see the adults, because Jan is outside in the garden, planting bulbs for next year, and Helen is sitting on the floor, making notes on a clipboard as she and three boys investigate a huge bag of conkers.

Beth stands and watches, with a wistful look on her face. She can remember being in the nursery, and even now, in Year 2, she sometimes misses the nursery and her favourite activities – the home corner, the writing area and the digging area outside where they grew the biggest sunflowers she had ever seen.

After a warm greeting from Jan, Beth puts her load of resources on the table, and slowly walks back across the room veering to the left to peep into the home corner at the children playing there. She closes the door on the nursery and saunters back along the corridor, looking at the displays as she goes. She turns towards her own classroom, and her step quickens as she remembers that she might miss her favourite lesson, Year 2 music with Mrs Carlton.

Beth epitomises many children in Year 2. She loves the challenge of being older, but she is already under pressure from the SATs tests that are looming on the horizon. She looks back with warmth at her early years, but she is excited and motivated by the opportunities that Key Stage 1 has offered.

Ruby is six

Let's look at another child, another school, and another Year 2 class for six and seven year olds, where the tensions are the same. Ruby is the oldest child of three. She has two brothers, Harry aged five and Paul who is two and a half. Her mum works as a part-time secretary for a solicitor, her dad works for the local council in the accounts department. The children have a childminder who looks after Paul for three whole days, and the older children before and after school. Harry and Ruby have breakfast at school, and Ruby goes to Gymnastics Club after school every Wednesday. She wants to be in the school gymnastics team, so she is working very hard at her exercises, sometimes showing these to the boys by bouncing on her bed, which gets her in trouble!

As the oldest child of three, Ruby feels a lot of pressure from her parents to do well at school and in sporting activities. They spend as much time as they can with the children at weekends, going out on visits to places of interest to the children, and helping them to follow up their interests with books, videos and discussions. Helping Ruby with reading has turned her into a fluent reader, but Harry is less keen, he would rather be playing with Lego.

Ruby's parents also want her to be a good example for her younger brothers, and this means she is expected to behave properly and help at home. They are also conscious that Ruby needs to do well in the national SATs at the end of this year, and their anxiety is putting pressure on her. Ruby is a bright, able girl, who works hard at school, and is making good progress, particularly in maths, but she lacks confidence and self-assurance. She seldom offers to answer questions in school, and when she is asked to show or talk about her work, she goes to pieces. This anxiety may well affect her when she is faced with the more formal assessment tasks, such as the spelling test, where she is under pressure.

It's lunchtime, Ruby has had her dinner and is on to the next thing. Today she has brought a bag to school, which contains her homework from the weekend. Their teacher asked the class to investigate Australia, and as Ruby's uncle lives in Australia, her mum helped her to collect up some of the things he has sent them since he emigrated. The bag contains a toy koala and a toy kangaroo, an ostrich egg (in a box), a map of Australia, a calendar of Australian animals, some paperweights and snow globes, and some postcards of Sydney, where her uncle lives.

Sunila and Ruby are in the cloakroom. Ruby says, 'Where am I going to put all this stuff? My mum made me bring it, and Mr Gordon'll make me stand at the front and show everyone. I'm going to hide it.'

Sunila looks in the bag and says, 'But this is really great! I wish I had an uncle in Australia. Look, there's a snow globe with a baby koala in it. All I could find was some pictures of kangaroos in my little brother's animal book, so I didn't bring it.'

'I don't care, I'm not going to show them,' says Ruby, and she hangs the bag on her peg with her coat over the top, and walks out into the playground.

Ruby is one of those children who has good ideas, knows a lot of things, but never puts her hand up or pushes herself to the front. She is a constant worrier, and her mum is very concerned that Ruby is getting increasingly anxious about school, and particularly about the SATs for seven year olds that she will be doing soon. Although Ruby is a good reader, and very good at maths when she has time to think, she often gets muddled when she is nervous, and this is a problem when she is reading the questions, as she rushes and gets things wrong. Her teacher and her parents have tried to reassure her so she can do her best, but this seems to just increase the pressure.

Sunila has been Ruby's friend ever since they were five, and knows that the more she pushes her, the worse she will get, so she just follows her out into the playground.

'Maybe you could just take one of the things in,' she says to Ruby's back, 'That koala looks really cute.'

At this point, Mr Gordon blows the whistle for afternoon school, and the children come in from the playground and sit on the carpet. Mr Gordon reminds them that they are going to start a new topic, and that they always start by making a mind map of what they already know. He has a globe on his desk, and he has pinned up a very big piece of paper, with an outline map of Australia, and he asks the children to work in talking pairs to write on sticky notes anything they know about Australia.

'Don't get your homework out just yet,' he says, 'We'll work in talking pairs first, so we can collect information and share what you already know.'

The children work in pairs to think about what they know, and write key words on sticky notes. Sunila is Ruby's talking partner, so they write about the things in Sunila's brother's book, not mentioning Ruby's uncle. When they have had some time to talk, the pairs make groups of six and share what they have found out. After a while, Mr Gordon asks the groups to place the sticky notes on the mind map to show what they know about Australian animals and birds, food, how people live, names of places, weather, music, art, seasons, etc. Each child reads what is on their sticky note as they stick it on the map, and sometimes Mr Gordon asks them where they found out the information. Most of the children have used the internet, some used books or asked their parents. Nobody says they have a relative living in Australia.

Ruby is really proud of the things she has brought, and in a way, she wishes she had brought them into the classroom but just thinking about having to stand up and talk about them makes her feel sick, so she says nothing.

When they have made the mind map, Mr Gordon shows them a short DVD about Australia, and the children discuss in their talking groups again about what else they want to find out, placing more sticky notes along the edges of the map. It's more difficult to talk about what you don't know, but the children are used to this sort of session and attack it with enthusiasm. Some of the suggestions are thoughtful, others show why it is important to find out about other countries: Do they play football? Is 'Neighbours' a real place? Where does Danni Minogue live? Do they speak a different language? Is it summer all the time? It's at the bottom of the globe, why don't they fall off the Earth? Do they have poisonous spiders there?

As they talk, Mr Gordon sorts their original knowledge into groups so he can make some learning challenges for groups of children to answer. In each challenge there are opportunities for writing, drawing, researching, calculating, but the central purpose of the challenges is to help children to collect information, to think, work together and present what they have found to the class. These are high expectations for such young children, but Mr Gordon arranges the groups carefully with leaders and followers, creative and mathematical thinkers, talkers and writers. He will match the challenges carefully to the groups of children, using some of their questions and some of his own.

Here are some examples of the challenges:

1. **Aborigines live in Australia**. What is an aborigine? Can you find some images of aborigine art? Could you make some aborigine art, using paints or collage?

2. **Australia in danger!** Research the Great Barrier Reef, and find out why it is in danger. Work together to make a painting, a collage, or a piece of music inspired by pictures of the Great Barrier Reef.

3. We know what sort of animals live in the UK. **What sort of animals live in Australia**? Work together to make two posters, one of Australian domestic and wild animals, and the other of British domestic and wild animals.

Ruby is in the group who are finding out about aborigines, and during the next hour, as they work on researching aborigine history and art, she sneaks out of the room and fetches the calendar that has some aborigine artwork on one of the pages, and a decorated boomerang on another. She is much happier sharing this information in a small group, and they are so enthusiastic about what she has brought that she fetches the whole bag, and shows all the things to her group.

Ruby's progress

Although lack of confidence is a continuing problem for Ruby, she is developing well within the normal range of ability for her age. Her language and mathematical skills are in advance of most of her peers, and she is one of a minority of girls who choose to follow a sport out of school. Her mathematical ability may well be inherited from her father, who is an accountant, and her literacy ability is not surprising, because, unlike Eli, she has been brought up in a literate household, where books are valued.

It is clear from the research evidence that children whose parents are well-educated do better at school. Their parents are more likely to be interested in what goes on at school, more likely to feel comfortable talking to teachers and more likely to help their

children with homework. All this will enable Ruby to learn more effectively, linking what she learns at school with experiences at home, where she has access to a family computer, and a room of her own where she can play and do her homework. The influence of her childminder is important too. Freda loves books, but she also has a great interest in art and crafts, particularly sewing and making cards, which she sells at the local gift shop.

Ruby's school

Ruby is fortunate too, in the school she attends. The head and the team who work with her, are willing to meet the challenges of continuous change within primary education in the UK. This change, often driven by political dogma, has resulted in a number of initiatives, including major revision of the primary curriculum, and the emphasis on evidence measures that could reduce the complexity of teaching and learning to numbers on a spreadsheet.

The teachers in Ruby's school welcomed the slimming down of curriculum subject content, but are more worried about the appropriateness of some of the expectations of children who are still very young. Some children in Ruby's class still only have a hazy idea of where some countries are in the world.

During their staff meetings, teachers have 'unpacked' the programmes of study for the curriculum, and repacked them by identifying the skills that need to be taught in each subject, giving time to these in more formal lessons. Then, where possible, the subject knowledge has been combined and organised into a series of cross-curricular topics or themes, where children can practise their thinking skills in researching and exploring topics that have interest for children of their age. Sometimes the topics are explored across the whole school, for example, a topic on the Olympic Games, culminating in a school Olympiad, and another called Our place, which explores local history.

The current topic for Year 2 is to explore information about a country outside Europe. The Australia theme addresses aspects of geography, design, art and technology in the National Curriculum for England, and of course, children will be using and extending their skills in English and mathematics.

While recognising the need to cover the National Curriculum, Mr Jordan, and the other teachers at Ruby's school, are really much more interested in how children learn, not just in what they learn. The methods they use to cover the National Curriculum are not just to teach children, filling their minds with empty facts that they regurgitate when questioned, or write about in empty tasks; they use the topic approach to make children think, solve problems, meet challenges, research and evaluate their own and others' work.

The questions and suggestions arising from the mind map encourage the children to use the key thinking skills:

- Information processing
- Enquiry
- Reasoning
- Problem solving
- Creativity
- Evaluation

There is a poster on the classroom wall that reminds the children of the importance of thinking, and they are encouraged to think about everything they do, to work together on projects and to evaluate how well their thinking has enabled them to answer key questions.

When he joins groups during their investigations, Mr Gordon tries to watch and listen to what is going on before he intervenes. He asks open questions that encourage children to respond at length, and at regular intervals, he encourages the children to share what they have found out, and help other groups with their challenges if they need it. Sometimes, individual children will leave their original group to join another, where their interest is captured, and this move is discussed and supported as a positive move, particularly when it involves one of the 'harder to motivate' children in the class. Mr Gordon knows the power of self-motivated interest to switch children on to learning.

He is also prepared to accept that some groups combine, others may become very interested in one small aspect of their investigation, and left totally 'cold' by others. He understands that children need to have their interest switched on, and this may happen by approaching the challenges through practical activities, such as making boomerangs or working at paintings inspired by aborigine art. Ruby, driven by her anxiety to be in control, usually starts by collecting facts and numbers. Sunila loves visual and creative explorations, so she will always begin with the 'making and doing' part of any task, researching only when she needs to, and often leaving painty finger marks behind her. The challenges in topic work give children opportunities to trigger their interest in activities geared to their learning styles.

Thinking skills

Even at the age of six and seven, these children are learning about thinking skills. They understand that they need both technical skills learned in more formal lessons, and thinking skills learned in cross-curricular projects. In English lessons they are taught about phonics, grammar, spelling, handwriting and other literacy skills; in mathematics lessons they are taught the skills of counting, calculating, sorting and ordering numbers; and other 'taught' sessions in music, science, PE, etc. include the teaching of important skills for learning. The timetable has fixed periods for core skills in English and mathematics, but is also flexible to allow for the teaching of specific skills in other subjects which may be needed for particular topics. When teachers observe the need to move children on in skills for music, history, geography or science they may use topic time to do this.

However, we all know that no matter how well these technical skills are taught, the children will need practice in active, enjoyable and stimulating activities that will make the learning permanent. Projects and topics provide an ideal jumping-off point for practice, where skills from many subjects can be combined. These involve the children in research, writing stories, poems and accounts, making up plays, composing music, presenting mathematical information and making books, posters and Powerpoint presentations.

Sunila, Ruby and their classmates are also able to use the topics as vehicles for counterfactual thinking. They make up and perform stories, write short plays, use puppets and small world characters, revisiting the things they are learning through whole-body activities. As children get older, they may not need to re-enact experiences by dressing up themselves. They can use counterfactual thinking in stories they write, by making up newspaper articles, or by manipulating puppets or other characters. Empathy for others, and imagining situations in different times and places becomes easier with practice, and then children appear to have less need of artifacts and props to express themselves as the people they are learning about.

Mr Gordon also plans periods where the children can enjoy using the resources they love as they explore the current topic. Paint, clay, sand, water, bricks and other continuous provision resources are provided in every class, up to Year 6. The teachers have carefully sequenced these materials and tools to make sure they encourage progression in children's thinking and learning, by enhancing simple resources with challenges. During the Australia project, children used construction materials to make models of the Sydney Harbour Bridge, paint and clay to produce works based on aborigine art, and craft and design techniques to make posters, leaflets and books.

At the end of each topic or theme, there is a celebration of what the children have learned. In this case, it will be a family barbecue, where songs, stories, food and music will be based on what the children have learned about Australia. Their work will be displayed in the classroom for parents and other family members to see, and Ruby's mum can take a photo for Ruby's uncle to show Ruby holding her work, and the souvenirs he had sent on display in the background. Maybe Ruby will have a chance to go and see her uncle, when they will have plenty to talk about.

Ruby still has to conquer her fears of the end of year tests, but working with other children, and honing her thinking skills will help her to be more confident in her own ability. Children like Ruby, who are sensitive to what others think of them, often do less well in tests. The cortisol manufactured by their bodies gets in the way of thinking at times of stress, and they freeze, unable to reach the links in their brains to the knowledge and skills they have. What a pity that so much emphasis is put on tests of what children can produce in exam conditions, with little recognition of the quality of work they can produce when their interest is sparked, where they have less pressure to produce simple answers to direct questions, and they have time to think and work together.

A message from Ruby

I may look quite grown up now, but inside, I'm still quite small, especially when I'm worried. I worry about a lot of things – what the other girls think of me, the SATs, having to talk in front of the class, whether I'm good enough to be in the gymnastics team, and loads more.

I like working in a small group, and really love it when Mr Gordon lets me work with my best friend Sunila. She's very funny and makes me forget about being worried. We are the green group, and we're a very good team. When we work on projects like the Australia one, finding things out, reading and looking on the computer – it makes learning easier and much more fun as we can decide how to work together to find the answers to the challenges, and then show our work to everyone as a group. We are all getting much better at using numbers and at reading because we need them for the projects, and Mr Gordon asks us every week to tell him about the things we've found difficult and he does special lessons on those things or gives us homework practice to help us.

Practitioners and teachers

- As children get older, we sometimes make assumptions about their maturity. We think that because a child is confident on a gym mat, they will be confident enough to talk to the rest of the class. How much time do you spend with children, looking at their strengths and weaknesses as well as their next step targets? How do you track the way children's learning styles change over time?

- At Ruby's school the teachers talked as a whole staff about approaches to a major curriculum change, and decided to adopt a combined approach with specific skills sessions and long periods for topic or project work where the skills could be practised through challenges. How do you discuss new curriculum initiatives, and decide how you are going to handle them?

- Themes and topics are one way of covering the curriculum in a way that interests children. Have you tried this method? How successful was it for you?

For parents

- Children are more aware of what you are worrying about than you might imagine. Try to keep your worries to yourself, particularly as the time for SATs or other tests approaches.

- Showing an interest in your child's learning continues to be important, even though they probably insist on walking to and from school on their own or with friends. Talk to your child about what they are learning, make the effort to attend parent consultations, and email or phone their teacher if you are worried about anything. Teachers are busy people, but they will welcome a dialogue with you about your child, as long as you don't become obsessive!

Interlude 6 It's not my style: learning styles and thinking skills

'Ultimately, there are two kinds of schools: learning-enriched schools and learning-impoverished schools. I've yet to see a school where the learning curves of the youngsters are off the chart upward while the learning curves of the adults are off the chart downward, or a school where the learning curves of the adults were steep upward and those of the students were not. Teachers and students go hand in hand as learners – or they don't go at all.'

Richard Barth, educator

'If we value independence, if we are disturbed by the growing conformity of knowledge, of values, of attitudes, which our present system induces, then we may wish to set up conditions of learning which make for uniqueness, for self-direction, and for self-initiated learning.'

Carl Rogers, psychologist

When Ruby and Sunila were embarking on their challenges in their Year 2 classroom, they both knew instinctively where they needed to start. If asked, they can both tell you what they like doing best at school, and how they like to learn. Ruby will say that she likes working from books and the internet, finding facts, figures and definite answers. Her favourite lessons are maths, where the answers are either right or wrong, and gymnastics or games, where the rules are clear and usually everyone follows them. When she was younger, her favourite occupations in the nursery were tidying up the book corner, so all the books were straight and in size order, putting away the wooden blocks in their special shelving unit, where they would only fit in one way, or making little books for stories with careful and detailed pictures that she took home to read to Harry when he was a baby. She is a logical-mathematical learner, with strong spatial skills that enable her to remember patterns and shapes.

Sunila, on the other hand loves art, music and drama, where she can have the freedom to experiment, create and work with others. She also loves playing with words, making up poems, songs and plays, and performing these with friends in the playground. She enjoys freedom and flexibility in activities where there aren't too many rules. When Sunila was in the nursery, she was always in the home corner or the craft area, making things, painting or drawing, usually in collaboration with other children, or at least, talking to them as she worked.

It may seem surprising that such different children can be such good friends, but they seem to complement each other perfectly, and when they work together they often come up with great ideas, as Sunila lets her creativity loose, and Ruby does the research.

Learning styles

Until recently there was a tendency in some schools to let learning styles become so dominant that children were pigeon-holed into one style or another, and unable to grow by experimenting and developing additional abilities. This could become a restricting factor, with children limited by being treated as either a visual learner or a kinaesthetic learner.

However, it is true that individuals have different learning styles. Consider how you learn best. Do you like to be shown, or to find out for yourself? Are you good at researching on the internet or would you rather listen to an expert or read a book? When you bring home a 'flat packed' piece of furniture, do you start immediately, or read the instructions? Do you use a recipe book, or make it up as you go along? We all learn in different ways, and learning styles are now agreed to be tendencies, not manacles, and every reader will be able to see that their own learning ranges over many different styles during the day, using different methods for different tasks.

Some of the methods which have been used to describe and classify learning are:

- VAK or VARK – visual/auditory/reading or writing/kinaesthetic – learning styles
- Multiple intelligences
- Thinking skills

Each of these has its followers, and each has its strengths and weaknesses as does any approach, particularly when it becomes a rigid mantra. There is a wealth of literature on these, but it will be helpful here to briefly remind ourselves of the key features of each one.

VAK or visual/auditory/kinaesthetic

Visual learners

Visual learners seem to come in two types: linguistic and spatial. Learners who are visual-linguistic like to learn through written language and reading and writing tasks, they will remember what has been written down, even if they do not read it more than once. They like to write down directions and pay better attention to lectures if they watch them. Learners who are visual-spatial often have difficulty with the written language and do better with demonstrations, charts, visual clues, pictures, objects, videos and other visual materials. They easily visualise faces and places by using their imagination and seldom get lost in new surroundings. They enjoy puzzle building, reading, writing, understanding charts and graphs. They have a good sense of direction, like sketching, painting, creating visual metaphors and analogies (perhaps through the visual arts), constructing, fixing, designing practical objects and interpreting visual images.

To support this style in the learning environment you could:

- Use charts, illustrations, concept maps, agendas, or other visual aids.
- Make sure you remove distractions from the area round the person speaking (and in the area round whiteboards or flipcharts).
- Let children draw simple reminders in pictures or words.
- Use whiteboards or clipboards for notes or individual mind mapping.
- Let children imagine the topic or encourage them to act out the subject matter.

Auditory learners

Auditory learners tend to learn through listening, they have highly developed auditory skills and are generally good at speaking and talking to groups of other children. They tend to think in words rather than pictures and like talking things through and listening to what others have to say. Auditory learners enjoy speaking, writing, storytelling, explaining, using humour, understanding the syntax and meaning of words, remembering information and arguing their point of view. They may talk to themselves, or move their lips when they read, finding it difficult to read silently. They may have difficulty with reading and writing tasks, and often do better working with a talk partner or using a tape recorder or Dictaphone, and listening to what was said.

To support this style in the learning environment you should:

- Speak clearly and make sure these learners are near to you, as hearing you is important.
- Reduce noise levels in the room.
- Let children sit in spaces where there are not too many visual distractions.
- Use rhyme, rhythm and word play in stories.

Kinesthetic learners

Kinesthetic learners also appear in two forms: those who learn though kinaesthetic means (movement) and those who are sensitive to tactile experiences (touch). Both types of kinesthetic learners appear do best while doing, touching and moving. These children tend to lose concentration if there is little or no external stimulation or movement. When listening to an adult, they may want need to move their hands, and often use gestures when talking themselves. When reading, they may like to look at the whole page first, and then focus in on the details (get the big picture first). They have a good sense of balance and hand/eye coordination, but find it hard to sit still for long periods and may become distracted by their need for activity and exploration.

To support this style in the learning environment you should:

- Use activities that get the learners up and moving.
- Play music, when appropriate, during activities.
- Let children move as they learn, give them physical breaks during activities when they need to sit and concentrate.
- Plan active exploration of the environment, with plenty of hands-on experience.
- Provide toys such as Koosh balls and play dough to give them something to do with their hands.
- Provide highlighters, coloured pens and/or pencils for note making.

Range of styles

In the past, some schools and universities went so far as to test children and young people at regular intervals, assigning them to one of the three types, and sometimes even planning activities, environmental factors and resources just to fit their learning style. This has proved to be counter-productive, as children regularly use more than one style during an activity, and need to use all their senses in learning, although one sense may dominate at different stages of development.

Babies and very young children are at a stage when they are predominantly kinaesthetic learners, learning with their whole bodies by touch. They also take in an enormous amount of information through their eyes, ears and even their mouths. The learning environment for very young children acknowledges this, and physical contact, visual stimulation, music and sound are central features in early years environments. There is even some concern that very young children are being presented with an environment that is *too* stimulating, causing some of them to shut down and stop learning.

As they grow older, the danger is that, because some children need less stimulation by touch, and can cope with more information presented in words, that teachers reduce the hands-on resources and activities, just when some children realise this is how they learn best! By the time children are in the later years of primary school, and particularly in secondary schools, classrooms can seem sterile and lacking interest as the focus moves to learning through listening, and active learning is limited to subjects such as technology and science. At the far end of the scale, some students at university are often expected to learn entirely by reading and listening, with little acknowledgement that many still need kinaesthetic or visual stimulation.

Jobs and professions have a hierarchy dominated by the culturally favoured learning styles – with practical activities remaining at the bottom of the ladder and intellectual ones at the top. However vital a plumber might be as your kitchen floods with water, she is still considered to be doing a less 'cerebral' job than a philosopher. Her practical skills need just as much brain-power, just used in a different way.

Useful techniques

Once you have identified which VAK techniques you use most frequently, there are some 'tricks' for you when studying or reading. They apply to children too. Ruby and Sunila use some of these preferences when they learn.

Visual learners

If you use visual learning techniques yourself, you will learn best in a visually stimulating environment, rich in pictures, patterns and colours, and in bright light. Because vision is important to you, you quickly remember places and positions, and remember things better if you are shown how to do them. You prefer diagrams and pictures to words or spoken instructions, and may say, 'Let me draw it for you,' when trying to explain something or show directions. If you use visual techniques, you learn best when you use pictures, objects or other visual clues. When reading or researching in books, you may take more notice of the pictures, using pictorial cues, and you may learn new words by using a 'whole word' approach to remembering the shape of the word. Your visual skills may have helped you to become a good speller. Mind maps, diagrams and pictorial recording are helpful for thinking, planning and remembering.

Auditory learners

If you use auditory learning techniques yourself, you may benefit from more traditional methods where information is conveyed in words and teachers talk to you more than showing you objects and pictures. The teacher's voice, tone and inflection will have had a big effect on how much information you retain. Auditory learners are often distracted by the use of objects or props and you may even close your eyes or look away to prevent yourself from being distracted from what a teacher is saying. When reading, auditory learners usually listen carefully to sounds, become good at using phonics and will break a word up into the component sound parts. Music can help you to concentrate, and you will probably learn well from discussion and talking.

Kinaesthetic learners

If you use kinaesthetic learning techniques yourself, you need to touch and handle objects you are learning about, and children will often listen better if they have a small object in their hands to manipulate. If you are a kinaesthetic learner, you probably learn best in an apprenticeship approach, where you can learn from copying someone else. When reading, children may trace the letters or explore parts of a picture with their fingers. You and kinaesthetic children learn much more successfully in laboratory-like situations where you are active and can handle the objects you are learning about.

Different styles

It is thought that 35% of us are predominantly visual learners, 25% are predominantly auditory learners, and 40% of us are predominantly kinaesthetic learners. However, it is rare to find a child or an adult who only uses one style.

Finding out your own preferences for learning is useful, and if you watch your own behaviour for a relatively short time, you will be able to find out which learning styles you appeal to most in your teaching. Some people have a distinct leaning towards one of the three, some combine two, and others seem to use all three equally. This is in some ways the ideal. Responding to visual, auditory and kinaesthetic stimuli will offer a greater chance of experiencing and retaining information, and the best teachers combine their teaching techniques to allow children to experience all three styles.

Multiple intelligences

The second way to look at the unique learning characteristics of individuals is to use the categories that Howard Gardner developed and refined over more than 20 years. This classification is usually referred to as the seven (or eight) intelligences. Gardner was very aware that some of the intelligences, or talents, that children have are under-valued by adults. Literacy, numeracy and oracy, the ability to read, write, calculate and speak fluently are highly valued by society, but skill in playing games, relating to other people, and enjoying or performing music or the arts, are often thought to be of less value. Gardner called all these skills 'intelligences', and believes that every person has all the intelligences in different proportions. Someone might be highly intelligent musically and linguistically, but less intelligent in physical or mathematical areas.

Western education loves the passionate musician or the great sportsman, but to really be respected by the most powerful people, the way to lasting success and a high position in society is through linguistic intelligence, interpersonal intelligence (the ability to get on with and influence people) or through mathematical intelligence.

When developing this theory, Gardner thought the intelligences should be described as:

- **Linguistic intelligence**, the ability to speak with conviction and use language to communicate well with others. Linguistic intelligence usually allows a child to learn to speak and read at an early age, learn another language with ease, and enjoy and experiment with words and sounds. Writers, poets, lawyers and speakers are among those that Howard Gardner sees as having high linguistic intelligence.

- **Logical/mathematical intelligence** shows itself in an ability to analyse problems, and remember patterns and sequences, and a real feel for what is orderly. A child with logical/mathematical intelligence will make links in their learning, allowing them to connect ideas. This intelligence is most often associated with scientific and mathematical thinking and logical/mathematical intelligence is not simply about being good at maths, as some people with this ability are not very good at numbers! In Howard Gardner's words, it entails the ability to detect patterns, reason deductively and think logically.

- **Musical intelligence** often shows itself in an unusual ability to sing, to recognise a tune, and to copy sound patterns. These children love singing, dancing, playing instruments and conducting others. Their sense of rhythm often makes it easy for them to learn to read. According to Howard Gardner musical intelligence runs in an almost structural parallel to linguistic intelligence.

- **Spatial intelligence** involves the potential to recognise and use the patterns of wide space and more confined areas. Blocks, maps and structured diagrams help these children to think.

- **Bodily kinesthetic intelligence** entails the potential of using one's whole body or parts of the body to solve problems. It is the ability to use mental abilities to coordinate bodily movements. Howard Gardner sees mental and physical activity as related.

- **Interpersonal intelligence** enables us to communicate effectively with others. Children with good interpersonal intelligence make friends easily, they listen to others, and empathise by saying kind things and looking after younger or more vulnerable members of the class. Amy and Keira showed their interpersonal intelligence as they looked after Eli on his first day. Educators, salespeople, religious and political leaders and counsellors all need a well-developed interpersonal intelligence.

- **Intrapersonal personal intelligence** enables us to look at our own behaviour, and understand ourselves to appreciate our own feelings, fears and motivations. Ruby knows she finds it really difficult to speak in front of the whole class, so she hides her Australian collection in the cloakroom. With help and growing maturity, she may be able to conquer these fears. In Howard Gardner's view it involves having an effective working model of ourselves, and to be able to use such information to regulate our lives.

- **Naturalist intelligence** was later added to Gardner's list and is agreed by him to be relevant. It is demonstrated in children who love being outside. They will collect objects and minibeasts to examine and are keen to share their interest with others. These children and adults also enjoy making dens, joining in Forest School activities and camping.

As with other personal and learning preferences and abilities, we all have a mixture, but will probably major in one or two. The child who has good interpersonal and linguistic intelligences may grow up to be a TV reporter or a politician. A child who is has intrapersonal and naturalist intelligences may grow up to be a wildlife photographer or explorer.

Teachers tend to have good linguistic and interpersonal intelligence, and if they are specialists, they may have good musical or mathematical intelligence too.

Thinking skills

More recently, educators and teachers have explored the range of thinking skills that children need, alongside their personal preferences and learning styles, to engage with learning. Learning by rote is only suitable for a very small number of specific collections of knowledge, such as multiplication tables, irregular spellings, or the kings of England. However, when you are embarking on learning something new, such as the Australia topic in our example, you need a different set of skills, which Ruby and her friends are becoming familiar with.

In her class, thinking about thinking, or metacognition, is an activity that everyone in the school is used to. From their earliest days at the school, children are used to having adults alongside them as they play and work, talking, asking questions and posing challenges and thinking problems. This activity, called sustained shared thinking, is at the heart of the early years curriculum in England, and in the latest guidance, Critical Thinking is included as one of the key CELs.

The advice for children and adults is that children should be:

Having their own ideas

- Thinking of ideas
- Finding ways to solve problems
- Finding new ways to do things

Making links

- Making links and noticing patterns in their experience
- Making predictions
- Testing their ideas

Choosing ways to do things

- Planning, making decisions about how to approach a task, solve a problem and reach a goal
- Checking how well their activities are going
- Changing strategy as needed
- Reviewing how well the approach worked

Adults should be encouraging young thinkers by modelling being a thinker, using the language of thinking and talk about strategies for thinking. And adults should provide plenty of opportunities and time for thinking, acknowledging that thinking takes time and support.

Learning environment

This guidance gives a clear framework for the learning environment for the youngest children. However, in the UK, when children reach about the age of five, they enter primary schools, and here the guidance on developing thinking skills is less clear. Instead of a heavy reliance on the environment for learning and how adults can be influential in this environment, there is a focus on the child. Children are expected to become much more aware of their own thinking, discussing the learning process, and understanding far more clearly the ways in which they can collect, interrogate and organise information, and present this so their own learning is confirmed and others can benefit from their work. The language of thinking is used in discussions, and the adult, through thoughtful and open questioning helps the child to understand what they are learning and to know more about the process.

Children won't get very far without the skill to organise and think about what they learn, and at the heart of this is metacognition: the ability to think about thinking and talk about thinking. There has been much work on thinking skills for children of primary age, and the work done in Northern Ireland, through The Education Department of Queen's University, Belfast, where Carol McGuinness has been influential in promoting thinking skills in schools. In 2013, the University launched a 'Teaching Thinking Network'. This work has been particularly helpful in unscrambling a complex subject.

The National Curriculum for Northern Ireland has structured its guidance according to the Thinking Skills and Personal Capabilities, which are at the heart of the Queen's University work:

- Managing information
- Thinking, problem-solving and decision-making
- Being creative
- Working with others
- Self-management

In their continuing work, Queen's University have provided a range of supporting documentation, including the following strategies for creating a thinking classroom, which are useful when evaluating practice. I have linked these to the practice in Ruby's school, where the teachers have discussed and adopted a thinking skills approach:

1. Set open-ended challenges

Real thinking skills come about by exploring your own learning, and to do this, children need to explore and search for meaning themselves, rather than having a 'right answer' to a challenge or problem. Ruby finds this difficult, as she would always rather have the correct answer in mind when tackling a problem. Her interest and ability in maths follows this pattern, and even in this subject she would rather work on calculations than problem solving.

Mr Gordon tries to follow the advice on thinking skills by encouraging children to come up with reasons for their decisions, offer possibilities as well as simple solutions, respond creatively to the challenges, value the different skills, views and abilities of members of their group, and develop autonomy, not just independence. Autonomy implies that the adult is on hand to support the children; independence may imply that the children are left completely on their own to succeed or fail without adult support.

2. Make thinking important

If teachers want children to think that thinking is important, it must be given space and time. Mr Gordon, and the rest of the staff in the school, make sure that the children have uninterrupted time and sufficient space to follow the challenges they undertake in group work. They also remind children often to take time to think and talk about thinking, using the language of thinking – might, perhaps, think, maybe, analyse, speculate, compare, research, predict, evidence, hypothesis etc. The posters and reminders around the school also help children to think, both inside the classroom and around the school. For example, rules are expressed in positives, such as 'Please walk', rather than 'No running'; or 'Please keep our playground a pleasant place', rather than 'No litter'.

3. Use effective questioning

The teachers know that open-ended questions are more likely to make children think, but they also know that children need thinking time before they answer. They follow the 'Question, wait, wait some more', method, trying to give children the ten seconds or more of thinking time, which is rarely given in our schools.

4. Make thinking explicit

If you are a teacher, making your intentions clear. If you don't tell children what you want, how can you expect them to achieve it? Mr Gordon and his colleagues know that a simple objective may not give children enough guidance to successfully complete the task. Teachers need to give children some information about the skills they will need to be using to learn, and the criteria for your assessment. As the Queen's University guidance says – 'Thinking is invisible. It needs to be brought into the open and talked about.'

5. Enable collaborative learning

Working together has been a common method for working in primary schools across the world, although some teachers have only a hazy understanding of how and why it works. The social benefits are obvious, and many girls in particular enjoy collaborative working, but there are cognitive benefits as well. Generating and discussing ideas encourages thinking and consideration of different perspectives, and developing the skills of joint decision-making will benefit children for the rest of their lives. Even disagreement and argument are features that contribute to collaborative working.

Ruby and her friends are used to working together in groups, and the groups change regularly so she gets to know the skills and personality differences of all the other children in her class. Mr Gordon encourages the groups to assign duties such as scribe, team leader, fact finder, creative director etc. to members of the group, and will sometimes makes life more challenging for a group by purposely leaving them without a natural scribe or even a team leader. He knows that there are some children (Danni may be one as she gets older) who assume the right to be team leader while others in the group are overlooked; or a group without a natural scribe may find other more innovative ways of presenting their work through IT, graphics or other media.

6. Promote independent learning

Although group work is highly regarded in Ruby's school, the teachers are also aware that children need to become independent learners in their own right, without relying always on a group of friends to motivate their learning.

Knowing your own skills, and abilities, as well as your weaknesses is a gradual process, and this is built up over time through regular self-assessment tasks and evaluations, both of group work and individual progress.

Ruby knows she is a good planner, and her friend Sunila knows she would always prefer to do things creatively. Both girls have set their own targets for learning, related to promoting the skills they already have, and working on those they need to nurture or practise. Mr Gordon will help them by looking carefully at the activities he plans, sometimes giving Ruby a more unstructured task, or Sunila one where she doesn't have the option of a creative presentation. Over the year, he will help the children in his class to develop as independent learners who are also aware of their own learning and metacognitive skills.

7. Make connections

Making connections between one subject and another, or between skills learned in one lesson and another does not happen automatically. One way to help children to understand how one area of learning affects another is to work through topics and themes for some of the time. This enables teachers to be explicit about the links between the skills taught, for instance, in literacy and mathematics lessons, and the application of these skills in real-life situations, through regular group work in cross-curricular learning.

Learning the alphabet can feel like a pointless activity until you need it to look up a number in a phone book; practising handwriting skills can be boring until you need to help your group to present their findings on a poster; learning tables needs practice in real-world challenges where miles need to be converted into kilometres or a journey time presented in the 24 hour clock needs to be converted into hours and minutes of flying time.

The teachers in Ruby's school understand that children need them to be explicit about the purposes of learning such skills, and need plenty of opportunities to use them, otherwise rote learning of skills remains just that – a sterile activity learned under the direction of adults and with no real purpose except to fill the school day.

Learning goes beyond just collecting and representing information into a much more complex set of skills, and as the children move into the older years of primary school, the teachers in Ruby's school help them to be more specific about thinking skills, by analysing and organising the complex skills involved in thinking about thinking.

Children learn that they need:

- Information processing skills – skills that will help them to collect, sort and organise information.

- Enquiry skills – that help the children to ask and answer questions in more complex ways than just closed forms with 'yes/no' answers.

- Reasoning skills – skills that help us all to think and reason, rather than just accept what we read or are told.
- Problem solving skills – skills that help people to recognise problems and to think about solving them.
- Creative thinking skills – skills that help us to think of alternatives and be creative about solving problems or finding solutions.
- Evaluation skills – skills that will help them to look at information and decide whether it is useful, discarding less useful information.

Effective thinkers and learners use all these skills, and the children who work with Mr Jordan are lucky in having a thinking adult and a thinking school to lead their learning.

Points to ponder

- Although we now recognise that a slavish adoption of one or another of the learning styles analyses described in this interlude is not a very useful technique, they are still useful background to teaching and learning. Do you use your knowledge of learning styles and thinking skills to help you to plan challenges and provocations to provoke children's thinking?
- Thinking skills approaches have been adopted by many schools to help children to learn about learning, and think about thinking. Wherever you are on the continuum between 'We don't use that stuff here', to 'We have made a good start and know there are many benefits to this', is there something in this interlude that you could incorporate in your current practice?
- Queen's University, Belfast, The University of Exeter, TASC, and Philosophy for Children, have all influenced the work on thinking skills in primary education, and are worth considering. Has this work any relevance for the future development of your school?
- In Ruby's school the teachers have decided to implement a version of thinking skills that they feel fits their work, and this includes giving time to thinking about thinking with and by all the children. How much time do you give to metacognition (thinking about thinking) in your school?

Stage 7 Into the pressure cooker – Dewain is seven and a half

'Nobody works better under pressure. They just work faster.'
Brian Tracy, motivational speaker and author

Dewain is seven and a half

Dewain moved into Mrs Bennet's class at the beginning of last term. It is now February, and Mrs Bennet is checking the children's targets for the first half of the year (September to February) before agreeing the next set, which will take the children to the end of the school year. There are no formal national tests (SATs) this year, so tracking the children's progress is even more important.

In this school, the children and their parents are always involved in the process. There has just been a parent's evening, and Dewain's mum, Iris, came with him to talk to Mrs Bennet and Mrs Shah (the teacher who runs the Nurture Group). Dewain has been attending the Nurture Group twice a week since October, after a fortnight during which his behaviour was so disruptive that he had to be removed from the classroom on several occasions to work outside the head's room. Dewain isn't violent or rude, but he is a clown. He finds reading and writing difficult, doesn't enjoy it, and instead of getting on with his work, he fools around, making faces, drawing cartoons in his books (he is really good at drawing) or distracts other children. He is never still, fidgeting and wriggling on his chair or on the carpet. Even when he is sitting in a group at a desk, his feet and legs are on the move, in unconscious jiggling and tapping

Despite his constant moving and fooling about, Dewain is a likeable boy, popular with adults and other children. He is small for his age, plump, and with a very beguiling grin, and shining eyes the colour of conkers, both of which he uses to charm his way out of trouble. This worked well with his previous teachers, but Mrs Bennet knows that from now on, if he doesn't settle down and work harder, it will be too late for him to catch up on all the time he has lost. The years in upper primary school are vital, and he must build on his recent progress or when he moves to secondary school, he will go under. He is one of those boys with potential but not much desire to learn – the *skill* but not the *will*! Mrs Bennet will have her work cut out to change him, but she really loves the challenge of working with boys like Dewain, and she knows that Iris, his mum, is a strong and supportive woman.

Mrs Bennet starts the conversation. 'Well, Dewain, let's have a look at your last lot of targets. How well do you think you have done?'

Dewain wriggles in his chair, and his mum says, 'Sit still!'

'I 'ent done bad with the writing 'ave I? And the reading. I did well wiv that book about the dog, din't I? That was good.'

'Yes,' says Mrs Bennet, 'We are very pleased with your work in English, and your brother has been helping you with your maths hasn't he?'

'Yep, wiv me tables. I can do up to nines now wiv no mistakes.' Dewain says proudly.

'But what about the other targets, the ones for your work in Eagle Club with Mrs Shah?' Mrs Bennet turns to Mrs Shah, who looks at Dewain.

'Let's go through them one at a time,' she says. What about – '**I will not interrupt adults and other children when they are talking**'?

Dewain looks at the floor. 'I'm trying, but not so good,' he mumbles.

'How about – '**I will listen to teachers, so I don't have to keep asking what I'm supposed to be doing.**' This is one of Dewain's real problems. He is so busy thinking about smart things to say that he doesn't listen, and never knows what he's supposed to be doing, so he bothers the other children to try to find out.

Dewain leans on his mum for support, but she is not responding, so he says quietly, 'I 'ave to stop asking Lyndsey what you said. I still don't listen prop'ly.'

'So, what do you think we should do about these targets? Can we change them? Can we do anything to make them easier for you?'

Iris, Dewain's mum, speaks. 'I have the same trouble at home, with the interrupting and the not listening, and we've thought of a trick. Maybe he could try it at school, it might help. Tell them Dewain,' she says, nudging him with her elbow.

Dewain mumbles, 'At first I 'ad to put me finger across me lips when she was talking, and that was OK, but I felt a right fool, so Mum let me put me finger on me belly button instead, and that works!' says Dewain, bursting out laughing.

All the adults laugh too, the tension eases, and Dewain agrees to try the 'belly button' reminder at school – through his shirt of course!

Mrs Bennet asks Mrs Shah, 'Do you think Dewain is ready to come back to the class full time?'

'What do you think Dewain?'

'I think I'd better try the belly button trick in Eagle Club and in class and see if it works first,' says Dewain.

'I've got your mum's email address, so we can send her a message every week to tell her how you are getting on. OK?' says Mrs Bennet. 'Let's try it for four weeks and see how we get on, then we may be able to talk about coming back to the class full time.'

Mrs Bennet is an experienced teacher. She taught Dewain's older sister and brother, so she knows his mum well, and respects her aspirations for her children. She knows that having a parent with high aspirations is more important in success at school than money or your parents' education. Dewain's brother Marlon, now 15, tall and athletic, is doing well at secondary school, excelling in maths and science, playing for the local football team, and spotted as a possible Olympic standard swimmer. Kayleigh, is 11 and in her final year of primary school. She is dreamy and writes endless poems and songs, composing music for them that she practises on her guitar in her bedroom. Her interest in words has meant high standards in English and her quiet thoughtful nature has made her a good friend and member of her class. She works well in small group situations, but can also work on her own. She has been a part of the home reading programme to help Dewain to meet his reading targets.

Early intervention

These two siblings make a formidable act for Dewain to follow. He can't compete with Marlon's sportsmanship or Kayleigh's popularity and standards in English, so from a very young age, just after his dad left them, Dewain just acted the fool. When he was little, his clowning was rewarded by attention from his family and relatives, so he kept going. When he was in the nursery and Reception classes, there were plenty of opportunities for him to entertain his friends by dressing up, throwing himself around on the outdoor play apparatus, and 'doing turns' at group times, where he would entertain the whole class with lively and amusing accounts of what he had been doing. He always chose active play with other boys, running, jumping, rolling and tumbling, rarely still or quietly occupied alone. He didn't even really get involved in construction, Lego, or small world play, which boys generally enjoy.

Dewain's development

His teachers began to be really concerned as Dewain approached the transition to formal schooling in Year 1 at five years old. They focused on offering him opportunities to begin the reading and writing processes, out of doors as well as indoors, but he just walked away if it was free choice, or did the bare minimum in adult-led activities. He was amenable to talk, stories and role-play, but it was almost impossible to get him to put pencil to paper. He would wriggle, sigh, stick his tongue out of the corner of his mouth, wind his legs round the chair and eventually produce writing that looked as if it had been done either by a teddy bear or a spider. He struggled with phonics, learning to read the first books by a combination of guesswork, whole-word recognition and picture clues. When he moved into Year 1 he was still producing what his teachers referred to as 'have a go' writing – single letters, squiggles and random shapes, presented to them with a broad grin, unable to even tell adults what he thought he had written.

By the end of Year 2, with a lot of help and some intervention work in reading and writing, Dewain was able to produce short written pieces, and with support from his mum, who read to him, with him and for him at home every day, his reading level was just within the average for children of his age. However, his behaviour in class was still unpredictable and attention seeking. He couldn't concentrate on written work unless an adult was next to him, regularly nudging him and reminding him of the task.

Dewain is one of the children who teachers worry about most. His work in English and maths is within the normal range, and progress in maths has been excellent since Marlon took an interest in what his little brother was doing. However, there are still huge gaps in Dewain's skills – he appears to have good mathematical knowledge, and improving literacy skills, apart from phonics, where he still struggles – but he still lacks the will to apply himself.

His attention span is short, he doesn't listen carefully, and his behaviour is immature and demanding of attention. It has gone beyond 'charming' into 'irritating', and this is beginning to affect the work of other children as well as Dewain himself. Of course, Mrs Bennet could refer Dewain for special needs support, but in a climate of cuts and reduced central services, she knows that there is little hope of additional help. If Dewain was violent, mute, dyslexic, autistic, or with a range of other named disorders, there would still be many hoops to jump through even for low levels of support, and of course, Dewain is certainly not autistic, violent or mute!

Dewain's developing male brain

Mrs Bennet knows that boys are more likely than girls to have problems with reading. Many boys have not made enough of the right sort of links between their right- and left-brain hemispheres to make a solid start on reading before seven, and this is why the lists of boys with reading problems at seven far exceeds the list of girls. It is a pity that we can't wait longer for boys' brains to ripen.

Dewain is very well coordinated, from plenty of outdoor, physical play in the early years, but the fine motor skills needed for writing, and fine control of both his eyes in 'binocular vision' to focus on the shapes of letters and words, are still well behind many other children of his age, and he guesses wildly without using any of the cues and clues most children have learned by this age. His spoken language is well within the normal range and he has a good descriptive vocabulary, but Dewain's listening skills and powers of concentration are still poor.

Equal but different

There appears to be some evidence that boys' brains are substantially different from girls' brains, and there is evidence that natural levels of chemicals such as the stress chemical cortisol may be higher in most boys, making them likely to be more aggressive more active, and more likely to fidget. Girls have higher levels of oestrogen, making them more interested in and more caring of people. The growth rate of male and female brains is different, not better or worse, just different, and individual parts of boys' brains seem to develop more slowly than the same parts in girls.

Some people think this difference in development is entirely caused by the way we behave towards boys and girls from the moment they are born, giving more attention to girls, holding and stroking them more, and even talking to them more, encouraging the parts of their brains linked to listening and communication skills to develop. Boys, even baby boys, do not give adults as much eye contact as girl babies do, and girls do seem to be more switched-on to faces than anything else in their surroundings, encouraging adults to interact with them. The result of this two-way interest is that girls will spend more time with adults, and will get more feedback from them about their activities, both in verbal and non-verbal ways, encouraging them to build those vital links in their brains that are associated with language and personal relationships.

Meanwhile, boys often seem self-sufficient, even though as we saw in young Sam and weeping Eli, boys do suffer more from separation anxiety. Once they have settled, they naturally move away from adults and towards other boys, getting involved in complex physical play, which does not appear to need adults. If we are giving less attention to boys, and I have a feeling that we may be, then we should try to make sure that when children are in our care, in nurseries and schools, we do not perpetuate this habit. We should give boys and girls equal attention, even though some boys may not welcome physical touching or adult company as much as girls do. At first, boys may well be puzzled and even resistant to our presence if they are not used to it. They may suspect an ulterior motive that will lead them away from active play into writing and sitting still! But be persistent, spending time with boys in their boisterous play out of doors, or in building, Lego, model making and small world play will help you to know the boys better, while giving the important message that what boys do is interesting to the adults in school, most of whom are females.

As you watch the boys and girls in your groups, you will notice that there are many differences between the ways they use their brains, and there is now considerable confirmation in scientific and professional research: boys do use their brains differently, even when they are very young. The right brain is dominant in all children at birth and for some time after, however, girls explore the links through the corpus callosum to the left hemisphere sooner than boys, who tend to concentrate on making links between neurons in the separate hemispheres, and predominantly in the right. Seven-year-old boys are still dominated by their right hemispheres, they need to move to learn, and are frustrated by having to sit still. They use all their senses all the time, and need to touch, talk about and even taste what they are learning. Dewain is still spending much of his time exploring and building his right hemisphere. This of course means that boys remain in 'big picture' land, while the girls are already building the architecture for reading and writing, and are ready for this to start around their fourth birthday. Some boys, like Dewain do not reach this stage of readiness until after their sixth or even their seventh birthday. Dewain is just reaching the threshold of self-motivated reading as he passes into his eighth year, as indicated in his enthusiasm for a book he had really enjoyed reading.

Dewain's play choices

In the early years, boys tend to choose activities that do not involve adults, congregating with other boys in active play without much talking, just using the single words associated with superhero and other gross motor play, such as 'C'mon', 'Gerroff', 'Run', 'Let's go'. Girls will tend to congregate around adults, watching and copying them, learning the conventions of linguistic turn taking and picking up subtle messages from body language and expressions. In childhood, girls have better hearing than boys and will listen for twice as long as boys of the same age – at this stage, boys will tend to prefer active play out of doors, on bikes and climbing frames, and running, racing and tumbling (as we have seen with Dewain). Girls on the whole tend to play in closer groups, giving each other roles and talking together much more, inventing stories and situations where they can explore their interest in other people, both real and imaginary.

One physical difference between girls and boys is in their vision. Girls have more P cells in their eyes, which are linked to seeing colour, they see better in low light, have a better visual memory, and wider angle sight. On the other hand, boys have more M cells linked to moving objects, they see better in bright light, and will focus on moving objects and use this interest to communicate – sometimes throwing things to show attention or affection.

The teachers in Dewain's previous classes understood his need for whole body play, and the importance to him of friends and an audience for his constant fun and games. They were prepared to wait for his brain and body to mature, offering him the activities that develop fine motor skills, and modelling these in small group times, but not forcing him to spend long periods involved in these controlled activities. However, one of the possible disadvantages of a programme with long periods of child-initiated learning is that a few children like Dewain will never choose to get involved in some activities, and can miss the experience that they need most. This can result in pressure later when the child reaches the classes where concentration and attention are paramount, and the teachers and children are closely monitored to reach externally set targets.

At a time when attainment is valued over progress, and **what** children learn is more important than **how** they learn, children like Dewain can suffer. In such a climate, there is no time to wait for developing brains to reach the optimum state for more concentrated learning, and that may result in unacceptable pressure on practitioners and teachers in the early years to embark on formal teaching too soon, or for too much of the child's time. There is overwhelming evidence that a child's own interests and abilities are what fires learning, we must not ignore the individual while chasing a mirage of sameness.

So what can we do to help Dewain?

Dewain has the *skills* he needs to succeed, to reach his targets and to return full time to his class. What his teachers need to think about is how he can muster the *will* to work at reading, writing and particularly at listening skills and attention.

His family is one of the keys to success. His mum, with Marlon and Kayleigh will need to continue their work with him. Their interest is the greatest motivator, and keeping up the momentum on reading and maths skills at home will take stamina as Marlon's sports practice and Kayleigh's storytelling involve them more deeply and take up more of their time. Iris will be the keystone to success. She is a determined woman who usually gets what she wants, and she will use praise and gentle nagging to make sure her older children play their part in Dewain's success at school. She knows that if he doesn't get sorted out at primary school, he will suffer at secondary school.

Iris's family is of Jamaican heritage, and she knows from experience that black boys are at risk at school, particularly at secondary stage when they are three times more likely to be excluded than white boys of their age. In primary schools, no one is quite sure why, black boys are doing just as well as their white and Asian peers in academic subjects such as reading. However, after secondary transfer, again no one is quite sure why, something happens, and black children, boys in particular begin to fall behind. By the age of 16, and GCSE exams, black boys' attainment is well below the national average.

Whether this is due to street culture, peer pressure to think of learning as not 'cool', or teacher expectations of black children in school, is unclear. What is true is that many black children go to schools in deprived areas where pressures on staff result in high staff turnover and exposure to a lot of supply or agency staff who do not stay long either. Stability at home is very important for children in these schools, and Marlon has managed to escape this pressure with consistent support from his mother. His interests in sport have given him credibility among his peer group, and his hard work on academic subjects has resulted in good predictions for exams next year.

Setting targets

However, Iris knows that Dewain is a very different boy, and he may be more susceptible to peer pressure than Marlon was. They have three and a half years to get him up to speed in academic subjects, but the priority has to be helping him to manage his behaviour in school, so he can avoid the trouble that may result in exclusion. Three and a half years seems like a long time, but changing habits built up over years will take time and determination. Some of the key routes to success in setting targets are:

- Commitment: Dewain must make a commitment to any activities or programmes that the group agrees to.
- Small steps: Particularly at the beginning, any activities and targets must be explained and planned in small steps, with rewards or acknowledgements for each step.
- Manageability: The programme must be manageable, or it will fail. Too many targets, too much time commitment for Dewain, Marlon, Kayleigh, Iris or the teachers may risk failure and disappointment.
- Predictability: Whatever programme or activities are planned, they must be carried out predictably. Programmes like this often fail because the participants alter the rules, move the goalposts, or lose interest.

In other words, the targets and outcomes must be SMART:

- **S** = specific
- **M** = measurable
- **A** = achievable
- **R** = relevant
- **T** = time bound

Here are some of the activities and tasks suggested by people in the group, for use at home and at school, for the trial period of a month.

Activities at school

- Mrs Bennet is the one with the most difficult task! She has promised to monitor Dewain's behaviour when he is in her classroom, using the two targets agreed at the

Parent's Meeting. She will note every time he meets one of these targets by nodding to Dewain, who will have a card where he can mark the credits himself. At the end of the week these can be totted up so they can email his mum every Friday, and he will be entitled to an extra turn on the computer at break time every time he fills a row on his card. Dewain can use the 'finger on his belly button' technique if he likes, but this will not be part of the deal – the aim is to help him to manage his own behaviour. The targets are:

- I will not interrupt adults and other children when they are talking.
- I will listen to teachers, so I don't have to keep asking what I'm supposed to be doing.

- Mrs Bennet will also help Dewain and some of the other boys who are finding Year 3 difficult, with their need for movement, by watching for fidgeting and giving them something active to do – boys (and some girls) who have difficulty sitting still and attending to adults, often find it helpful to run round the playground, kick a ball against a wall, to do some simple exercises such as press-ups or star jumps, or some simple brain gym exercises just before they are expected to concentrate. This seems to get rid of some of the chemicals that are flooding their brains and making them restless. It won't hurt the more sedentary girls either, to oxygenate their brains regularly during the day.

- Mrs Shah has heard that there are some games Dewain can play at Eagle Club, to improve his concentration. She will collect some of these and give Dewain and the other Eagles time to play them. She will also lend some to Dewain to take home to play with his family.

  These games include:

- memory (or pairs)
- Kim's game (or say the missing object from a tray of objects)
- word and number searches or crosswords
- I-spy
- categories – players choose a category, such as children's names and take turns through the alphabet to say a name starting with each letter
- word tag – choose a category, and the first player says a word; the next player says a word starting with the *last* letter of that word
- jigsaw puzzles
- picture spot – looking for objects in pictures or a *Where's Wally?* book
- computer games available free on the internet which are intended to improve children's attention.

At home

For the trial period of a month:

- Marlon says he will help Dewain with his maths homework for 15 minutes a week. Mrs Bennet agrees to set the maths homework on Friday so the boys have to find 15 minutes together during the weekend, when Marlon has a bit more flexibility in training and homework. Marlon also says he will continue to help Dewain with mental maths – tables, number bonds etc. Dewain will have to agree to come for a training run with him once a week, so they can do the mental maths practice as they run. Dewain is delighted with both these suggestions. He really admires his older brother, and will love the time spent with him. It is interesting that many boys will listen and remember things when running or walking beside another person, sitting opposite and making eye contact seems to raise cortisol levels which get in the way.

- Kayleigh says she will help Dewain learn the spellings for the weekly spelling test. She will also help with the reading, by reading some stories to Dewain, starting with some by the same author as the dog story he enjoyed so much.

- Iris says she will continue to read with Dewain for at least ten minutes a day, either before he goes to bed, or before school. She's also heard that fish oil supplements sometimes help children's concentration, so she's asked Dewain if he will try these for a couple of months as there's a special offer at the local chemists.

This may seem a lot of targets, but note how everyone has a clear part to play. The only ones with recorded measures are the classroom targets, which have a record card, but ownership of this is clearly with Dewain. Each person has taken responsibility for managing and monitoring their own contribution, and for each of them, the load is reasonable. Dewain has agreed to try not to let anyone down, so hopefully, now he is older, he will be able to participate in these SMART targets and appreciate the effort everyone is making to help him.

The targets will be monitored in a month' time, when Iris, Mrs Bennet and Mrs Shah will meet with Dewain to discuss progress. They have arranged to take email, Twitter or telephone reports from Marlon and Kayleigh. They will each report on whether their contribution is manageable, and how well Dewain is responding.

The reward for all this hard work, and even at seven and a half, Dewain needs rewards, will be a family outing to their favourite restaurant, followed by Dewain's choice of a film.

Good luck Dewain!

A message from Dewain
(translated by his teacher to remove street slang!)

Hi there readers – here is my message.

I'm lucky. My brother can teach anybody anything, and my sister has written some cool plays for black kids and asked me to act in one. My mum is my mum, I won't have anything said against her, but she sure has a hard hand when she slaps you!

What I need to tell you is don't give up on us boys, we need you to believe in us, and with the help of someone like my brother we'll get there. But I've got some friends that 'ent so lucky, so make sure you find them, give them some time and believe in them, and they'll surprise you!

For practitioners and teachers

- Setting clear targets and agreeing them with the child and their family is time consuming, but rewarding when children like Dewain and their family take up the challenge. How do you manage the process of target setting in your school?

- Dewain's message is clear. How do you spot the children who need that extra bit of time, care and input, and how do you find time to arrange and implement it?

- The way that teachers, support staff and parents work together is one of the keys to success in supporting children like Dewain. How do you manage this complex task in your school or setting?

For parents

- Your support continues to be vital as your child moves into the older years of primary education. Are there any things that teachers could do to improve the meetings and other access to knowing what and how your child is learning?

- Dewain's mum is a good parent, who has worked hard to help her children to succeed. Could you use any of the ideas she had when working with your own children?

- Are there things that you couldn't do at school? How did you overcome these?

Interlude 7 Pay attention! Gaining and maintaining focus

'An expert is someone who has succeeded in making decisions and judgements simpler through knowing what to pay attention and what to ignore.'
Edward de Bono, physician, author, inventor and consultant

When we are not wishing that children would pay more attention, we are probably wishing that more children would pay attention!

The world is a busier, faster moving place than ever before, and it isn't going to slow down for us. In fact, it is predicted that the pace of change will continue and even increase. Children are bombarded by information wherever they go, and when not in school, the screens of phones, computers, tablets and gaming machines compete with each other and with us for attention. It is no wonder that children find it more and more difficult to listen and pay attention to a teacher, particularly if the teacher doesn't have an arresting costume, coloured lights and the current music style to back them. Teachers and parents have an increasingly difficult job helping children to focus their attention on what they want them to learn. Of course, as I have said many times in this book, it is much easier to capture the attention of anyone if we are focusing on something they are interested in. Relevance is the first trigger for attention, and we use this most of the time to attract the attention of babies and very young children. However, when we are working with older children, there are many occasions when we can't use Superman cloaks, puppets or Lego to ignite a thirst to learn multiplication facts or this week's phonemes.

Most adults have learned to screen out some of this information, although when the eyes of our partner, our best friend or a child constantly flick from our face to their mobile phone, from the real world to the virtual one, we are understandably irritated.

When we are teaching, or leading an activity with a group of children, there are hundreds of stimuli that could distract them – our new hairstyle, the pattern on the fleece of the child sitting in front of them, the weather outside the window, a nudge and giggle from a friend, or even the thought of what they might do once this period of enforced sitting is over. If the objective of the activity is explained to children at the beginning of the session, this may make things better or worse – 'Oh, good, a story,' or 'Oh no! Not mental maths again!' and setting the scene by careful explanation may make it clearer for an adult observer, but could immediately switch off a section of your audience.

Receiving and processing information

Let's look at what happens in the brain when a new experience, person or activity appears. In this situation, the brain has to filter out some of the incredible 400 billion bits of information it receives every second. The brain cannot be expected to process all this information, and we are only aware of about 2,000 of those bits. As you sit and read this book, your brain and body are dealing with huge amounts of information, without needing to bother your consciousness – you have automatic systems to manage breathing, blinking, pumping blood, processing waste or harmful chemicals, making glucose to feed your brain, producing bodily fluids, swallowing, etc. If your body didn't automatically keep your balance, using your eyes and the fluid in your ears, you would fall or slide from your chair. Information from the world outside your body is received and processed – is that a draught you can feel? Is that sound the familiar heating pipes or something new? It's getting dark, do you need to switch the lights on yet? You can feel whether you are uncomfortable, tired, hungry, thirsty, needing the toilet, but you don't think about these things all the time, your body and brain take care of them. That is unless one of these automatic systems goes into overdrive – perhaps you start to fall asleep and, as you start to snore, your brain wakes your consciousness; your system becomes dehydrated and you go for a wander to find water or wine; or your mobile phone beeps to signal a text and you lose attention while you decide whether to answer it. This tripping backwards and forwards from unconscious to conscious is automatic, and we can take it in our stride, although in some children these triggers come just too late to avoid an accident.

Reflective or reflexive response

But what happens if you are sitting reading this book and you see someone hop over the fence into your garden? It is someone you don't recognise. Your brain goes into overdrive. You must do something, and what you do will be governed by your emotions. You forget that you were hungry or thirsty, your brain and body start to manufacture stress chemicals such as cortisol and adrenaline. Your prefrontal cortex sends messages deep into the middle of your brain where the decision is made to act in one of two ways:

1   You could act in a reflective, analytical way to a new experience, staying in your thinking brain, and this is best if you have time, time to explore what is happening, compare it with previous experiences, and make a rational response. Perhaps it's next-door's gardener. Is it the window cleaner, climbing over because you have forgotten to unlock the back gate? Reflection and rational behaviour are logical, but they take time, and won't help if this is a burglar or an escaped prisoner on the run.

2   Or you could act in a more reflexive response. This is a more primitive process, aimed at helping you to survive, and is propelled by instinct and emotion. It's fast and exhausting

but it gets you out of trouble, at least initially, and is also the default mode. You start to breathe heavily, your heart races, and if you have read Interlude 2, you will 'lose control of your chimp', choosing to burst into tears, shout at the intruder, phone the police, or hide under the coffee table.

Under stress or when experiencing something new, we are programmed to take the second route – a reflex. This route takes us to the amygdala, which immediately sends messages throughout the brain to put the senses and the emotions on alert – breathing, heart rate, body temperature, blood pressure, go on 'red alert', you blush, sweat, shake. The experience is tagged as important and wired as an emergency. Other systems shut down and you suppress some less important sensations as you focus on the emergency. Fear is one of the most powerful reflexive responses, taking over your whole body, and fear is often associated with phobia triggers, irrational fears brought on by spiders, snakes, cockroaches, or even more rarely, objects as simple as buttons or clowns. Telling a phobic to calm down and act reasonably won't get either of you anywhere.

The part of the brain that controls reflexive responses and classifies new experiences as safe or significant is the amygdala, a small organ, shaped like an almond and in the middle of your brain, where the older parts of the brain meet the human cortex. The amygdala works to manage feelings such as aggression, fear, anxiety and worry. Fast and efficient connections with the frontal lobes that manage impulsivity, long-term planning, discrimination and fine judgement enable the amygdala to respond very quickly, triggering the three F's:

- flight (run away)
- fight (go on the attack)
- freeze (go into a catatonic state where you can't move, just like a rabbit in the headlights of a car).

These are all responses that involve the primitive parts of our reptilian brains. Reflective responses keep us in the cortex where we can think rationally as humans, but reptiles only have reflex responses, fight, bite or flight, they don't have the evolutionary advantage of reflection.

When children are presented with something that is new, frightening or that they know they can't do, their immature brains often go into just the same mode – they lose control of their chimps and we have all seen the result – the child who 'freezes' like a rabbit in the headlights (think of Eli), runs away (either actually, or by using avoidance techniques like Dewain's clowning, or Ruby hiding her souvenirs), or has a tantrum and becomes defiant (think of Sam's response when his dad was late).

Learning to be more relective

Very young children are more likely than older children to act reflexively, as their emotional responses develop before their ability to manage them. Boys are also at risk because their emotional centres develop more slowly than those of girls. Tantrums, defiance, weeping, hiding, and clowning are all reflex behaviours, and children who are still responding in this way to reasonable requests can be difficult to manage within a class or group. Even when children have time to reflect and come up with that reflective response to something new or threatening, their immature systems sometimes over-ride common sense.

How can we help these children to approach things in a more reflective way, so their behaviour does not get in the way of learning? Here are some ideas:

- Teach strategies for managing their own behaviour – counting to ten, deep breathing, closing their eyes may help to make thinking time.

- Discuss situations where children often lose their equilibrium – sharing a toy, waiting for a turn, spilling something, accidentally spoiling their own or others work. Use puppets or photos of unknown children to help recall the incident and don't embark on this while emotions are still high.

- Maintain a calm and accepting atmosphere, where children feel it's OK to have another go, admit you don't know, or ask for something to be repeated.

- Give children time to respond to you or others – remember the ten-second rule – it takes most children at least ten seconds to think and respond to a question. Don't let children like Danni jump in too soon, as this can lead to frustration.

- Give plenty of warning that something new or a change of activity is on the way.

- Demonstrate a new technique or skill yourself before expecting children to manage it.

- Make sure children are well fed and hydrated, with plenty of foods that make them resilient and enable them to manufacture serotonin.

- Avoid situations where children feel exposed, such as sharing their work with the whole class.

- Offer children opportunities to work in pairs or groups, this takes away the sense of exposure, and encourages collaboration.

- Have a discussion in private about the things an individual child finds difficult, and offer ways that you can help them to overcome these.

- Introduce new concepts and ideas in small steps, with pauses, gaps and rest between, and opportunities for 'no risk' strategies such as traffic lights, where children can say if they are not sure of new concepts or instructions, so they can be repeated.

- Establish systems such as 'traffic lights, where children can check or get more information before starting on a task.

- Remember the concentration calculation – on average, children can concentrate without a break on something they have not initiated themselves for about the number of minutes of their age in years (plus or minus a minute) – a five year old can concentrate without a physical break for about five to six minutes, an eight year old for eight to nine minutes. This does not mean a new activity, just a break for a chat, a movement, a stretch, or a song.

- Stay with them as they work. Children who are experiencing stress will concentrate much better if an adult is sitting near – in fact, most children will!

- Use children's existing interests as jumping off points for new ones.

The time it takes for the brain to make a really simple decision, such as naming an object or reading a word aloud, is about 300–700 milliseconds, which means that the brain can only make about two conscious calculations per second. However, this simple calculation is misleading, because a well-trained brain can make incredibly complex decisions much more quickly, and often makes these decisions without reference to our conscious thinking.

An apparently simple task such as paying attention to you when you speak, is a very complex and difficult task for a young child who has not yet learned to control the muscles for sitting still, or the skills of listening closely, when there are so many other distractions, which might include real anguish as they are pulled away mid-activity to do something else, or wondering whether their parents will have another argument tonight. We may never know what these are, because even if we stop and ask, the child may not be able to tell us. A bit of patience and understanding, and perhaps a bit more time to engage, may make all the difference between frustration for the adult and success for the child.

Points to ponder

- Paying attention is one of the key skills to success in learning for life. If children can maintain attention and concentrate they have much more chance of success later in school. How do you think we should proceed in this particular aspect of learning?

- Think back over the examples and the descriptions of children in the book. Have they given you an insight into the children you currently work with? Have you picked up any tips that might help you?

- If you could recommend one piece of advice that every parent should take, what would it be?

Conclusion

In this book I have tried to unscramble the complexity of learning in the early years, and I end by suggesting what each child might best benefit from as they embark on the next stage of learning to learn. With the help of seven children, I have looked at the research into brain development and how it affects our ability to learn, interspersing these with some deeper asides.

At the end of this process, I conclude that our gifts to the seven children should be as follows:

- Max, still in the womb, has everything to learn. His potential is enormous, and success depends as much on chance as on his genes or his upbringing. The best 'birth day' gift for Max would be for society to realise how much difference could be made by an investment in the nine months before birth and the early years of education. In the meanwhile, he needs to meet adults who are gentle, loving and interested in him, and in showing him the world.

- In Marta's treasure basket we should hope for her to find things that fascinate her interest, stimulate her senses, and give her a world to talk about, whether she chooses to talk in Spanish or English.

- Sam, that brain on legs, just embarking on the reality of nursery happening relentlessly every day, continuing year after year, has a loving family, but the gift he needs is to be himself, not what his sisters want him to be. In this way, he may learn to communicate clearly, able to say what he wants and what he wants to learn.

- Danni just needs more of the same, but preferably with continuing access to the dressing-up box of her imagination, where she will continue to be everyone she meets, learning about them by being me, being you. She is a sponge for information and experiences, soaking up everything school and her family can offer her.

- We all need to remember Eli, because he exemplifies what happens when a child doesn't have what they need: a supportive home background, a good diet, and a few treats. It would cost so little to support him, but so much to solve the whole problem of the children who live in poverty. School may be able to compensate for some of the things he lacks, but children like Eli, particularly in times of financial difficulty, are often the casualties of a toxic mixture of nature, nurture, culture and chance.

- Ruby, with a calm and well-ordered life is destined to succeed, as long as we can give her the gift of self-confidence to carry her over the hurdle of the SATs and into the upper years of primary education, preferably with the consistent support of her group of friends, and hopefully with the boost of success in the Gymnastics Club. Continuing in a school committed to a Thinking Skills approach will be an advantage to her too.

- And Dewain, lovable rogue and the bane of every teacher's life! We must wish him success in his targets – I will never be able to hear his name again without seeing his hand on his 'belly button' as he quivers with the need to tell his teacher what he thinks.

Seven children, with seven different histories and seven different sorts of learning needs. It is amazing that teachers succeed in finding the right match for so many, and that they so seldom give up trying with the others. The gift I would give to every child is that they find a teacher with the *skill* and the *will* to unpack their unique box of needs and work with them to find the answers.

I hope you find this book useful in your work with children, as you strive to maintain their right to learn in the way that suits them best.

'It is, in fact, nothing short of a miracle that the modern methods of instruction have not yet entirely strangled the holy curiosity of inquiry; for this delicate little plant, aside from stimulation, stands mainly in need of freedom. Without this it goes to wrack and ruin without fail.'

Albert Einstein, theoretical physicist

Bibliography

Asbury, Kathryn and Plomin, Robert (2013) *G is for Genes* John Wiley & Sons
Cummings, Dominic (2013) *Some Thoughts on Education and Political Priorities* The Guardian
DfE (2013) *Statutory Framework for the Early Years Foundation Stage*
Education Scotland *Pre-birth to Three: Positive Outcomes for Scotland's Children and Families* (2010)
Gardner, Howard. E. (2008) *Multiple Intelligences: New Horizons in Theory and Practice* Basic Books
Gurian, Michael (2010) *Boys and Girls Learn Differently* Jossey Bass
Peters, Steve (2012) *The Chimp Paradox* Vermillion

Index